CW01083539

Cycling End to End, the Wrong Way
John O'Groats to Land's End

Cycling End to End, the Wrong Way
John O'Groats to Land's End

Copyright © Trail Wanderer Publications 2020

www.trailwanderer.co.uk

contact@trailwanderer.co.uk

First Printed 2020

Printed ISBN 978-1-9160097-3-8
eBook ISBN 978-1-9160097-4-5

By Matthew Arnold.

Always take the scenic route.

CONTENTS

JOGLE Route

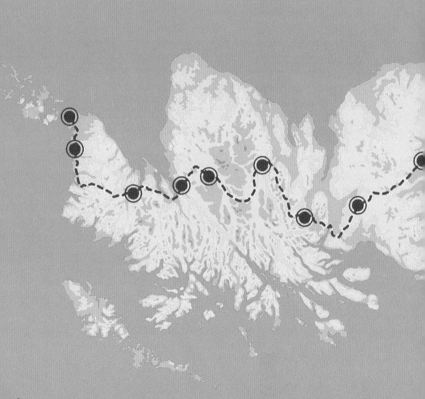

1. John O'Groats
2. Thurso
3. Crask
4. Inverness
5. Aviemore
6. Pitlochry
7. The Trossachs
8. New Lanark
9. Gretna
10. King's Meaburn
11. Forest of Bowland
12. Manchester
13. Bridgnorth
14. Gloucester
15. The Mendips
16. Exeter
17. Dartmoor (Brentor)
18. Veryan
19. Land's End

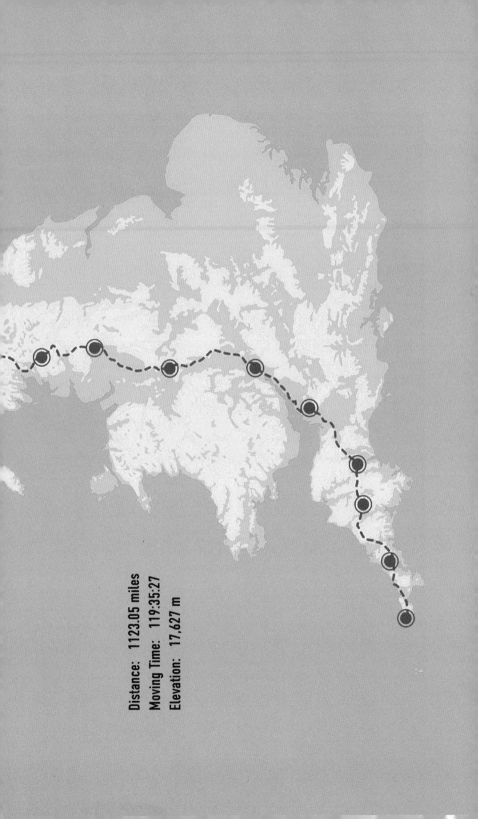

Distance: 1123.05 miles
Moving Time: 119:35:27
Elevation: 17,627 m

INTRODUCTION

Why would you want to cycle End to End?

Apart from a gap of a few years, I've always had some sort of love for two wheels. It all started in my youth with BMX since I grew up during the period when the popularity of BMX took a massive hold in the UK, with its peak probably reaching around the mid-90s. A fond memory of mine is heading out with my friends every evening and weekend - riding to spots around Exeter or hopping on the train and checking out the skateparks around Devon.

Eventually, I outgrew BMX before moving away from Exeter, which is when I lost interest in anything to do with cycling. It was only a few years before completing JOGLE that I rekindled my love for two wheels. I had bought my first ever road bike, and at first, I wasn't massively into road cycling, I just enjoyed heading out on a sunny evening blasting around the countryside. But I quickly recognised the fantastic benefits of having a road bike, mainly the sense of freedom it brings. Heading through places that you wouldn't normally encounter; you get to see the countryside in a whole different light - not to mention the positive effects that it has on improving your health and wellbeing.

For me, cycling End to End was all about the challenge of riding such a massive distance. I loved the idea of the adventure, to be able to look back on and say I have ridden one of the most iconic long-distance cycling journeys, to ride the entire length of the United Kingdom.

I instinctively thought of going from John O'Groats to Land's End. Being from Exeter, the city where I've grown up and still reside, it just made sense. There were two reasons for this. Firstly, I didn't fancy the monumental train journey home afterwards; I would prefer to get this out the way at the beginning. Secondly, the aspect of riding down through the country would seem like getting closer to home with each mile covered – providing a huge psychological boost.

My route would loosely follow the Official Land's End to John O'Groats Sustrans Guide. As this was going to be a big trip, I wanted to take a more scenic route, to take my time and make the most of the experience. My planning consisted of breaking the journey down into 18 days, as this was the maximum amount of time that I could get off work. Due to a limited budget and a desire to keep costs as low as possible, I also decided that I would wild camp various nights mixed in with a few nights of luxury staying in hotels or B&Bs (Although I still spent a fortune). That said, my trip would be completely self-sufficient, and I would be on my own.

PLANNING

Route

Whichever way you decide to cycle, planning your route is always a good idea. The shortest route is around 900 miles, and most people can comfortably do it in about 10-12 days, although to do it in so few days, you'd likely be riding on busy roads. But it depends on what you'd like to get out of your adventure.

I had the idea of wanting to take my time, to explore and see more of the countryside and visit places I hadn't seen before, rather than race to the end. I discovered the Official Sustrans LEJOG Guide, a guide covering nearly 1200 miles with lots of information including maps, directions, sites to see and accommodation; I thought it would be ideal. The route is broken down into 28 easily achievable stages - perfect if you have lots of time to spare. But since I didn't have 28 days, I condensed it down into 18 instead.

If you haven't heard of Sustrans, they are a charity responsible for the formation of the National Cycle Network and its upkeep. The network covers some 16,575 miles (26,675 km) and features a wide range of traffic-free paths and quiet roads. If you like, you can purchase their guide from their website for £14.95.

Admittedly at times, I did find it hard to follow, especially when passing through towns. Although, that may be because I can't follow maps properly! Regardless, I didn't entirely stick to the routes in the book as sometimes its trails involved a wide detour. Instead, I took more direct routes, so I didn't add any more distance on to my journey. By the time I got to Manchester, I had stopped using it altogether, instead preferring to use the cycle route planner on Google Maps to calculate a faster route.

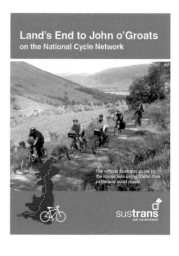

That said, the book is still an excellent resource for ideas when planning your route, as it takes you through some of the most picturesque landscapes in the United Kingdom. Plus, you'll be supporting a worthwhile charity by purchasing the guide.

If you would like the GPX files for the route I took, then you can download them by visiting my website at the following link.

www.trailwanderer.co.uk/jogle-planning

Accommodation

Accommodation is likely to be one of your most significant expenditures. After all, the average B&B costs around £80 for a night. And if you decide to complete the route in 10 days, this adds up to £800 - a rather substantial sum of money.

Ways to reduce costs are to use hostels and campsites. Hostels are dotted all over the country and are fantastic places to meet people. But don't forget that hostels fill up quickly, so you'll need to book well in advance. Likewise, you'll find campsites all over the place. A pitch for the night can be as low as under £10, depending on the time of year. So, it's well worth considering if you're looking to cut costs. Airbnb is another excellent alternative as it provides more flexibility on places to stay. Most of them are expensive, but you can find some good deals if you look around.

Prices tend to be at a premium on Fridays and Saturdays, but you can typically find hotels at slightly cheaper rates during the weekdays. Premier Inn is a fantastic option as they allow you to take your bicycle into your room. I got a great deal at the Premier Inn in Salford, Manchester, for example. Staying on a Sunday cost me around £41; well worth it for a night of luxury!

Below you will find a number of websites which I used to book my accommodation.

The Crask Inn
www.thecraskinn.com

Pitchup
www.pitchup.com

England & Wales YHA
www.yha.org.uk

Scottish YHA
www.hostellingscotland.org.uk

The Croft
www.crofthotelbridgnorth.co.uk

Premier Inn
www.premierinn.com

Thurso Bay Caravan & Camping park
www.thursobaycamping.co.uk

Nutrition & Hydration

Food is your body's energy, and you'll need to fuel yourself properly to cover the miles each day. If my stats are anything to go by, I was burning between 4000-5000 calories a day if not more - I certainly wasn't taking in that much! A lot of the time, I was running on empty - mainly powered by bags of sweets, cakes, and cans of pop. I would not recommend doing this!

I won't bore you with stats on calorie intakes and how much energy you get from certain types of foods. The main thing is that you consume as many calories as possible, and include a decent mixture of foods. Eat as much as you can at breakfast and have a large meal in the evening. I noticed the benefit of piling on the calories from my stay in Manchester. I wolfed down a three-course meal in the evening and an all you could eat breakfast the next morning. Thanks to this, I found it a breeze to smash out 88 miles to Bridgnorth the following day – in stark contrast to the day before!

If I stayed in accommodation, breakfast was always porridge and a fry up and any extras such as toast, fruit, or pastries to set me up for the day. I never really stopped for lunch as I wanted to get to the destination as early as possible. During the evenings, again, if I were in accommodation, it would be a large meal or a trip to a supermarket to pick up supplies.

On the nights that I wild camped; it was a combination of boiled rice along with a packet of tuna mixed in. An extremely bland choice of foods and didn't go down that easy. It's certainly not what you want when you've exhausted yourself from 10 hours in the saddle, craving flavoursome food!

As I took the scenic route down through the country, there were long periods I wasn't able to pick up food because of a lack of shops. But a large chunk of my journey involved passing through small sleepy villages, where the local village shop was my only option for gathering supplies. In many of them, there were also numerous local pubs, too. But I didn't fancy leaving my bike outside for long periods, so it wasn't an option for me for the most part.

There were a few occasions I passed a shop and said to myself; I'll stop at the next one. The problem was that when I arrived at the next one (which was often some distance away), it was closed. So, if you encounter a convenience store, it's worth stopping to pick up some supplies even if you don't think you need anything yet.

Keeping hydrated is equally important, I had three water bottles, one lost to the A9 and another deciding to jump out of its holder coming down a fast, bumpy descent never to be seen again. As a result, I had no choice but to replace them. Thankfully, I also had a 1.5-litre bladder in my backpack as a backup option. I got through an awful lot of water, getting very low a few times. And although I didn't have any with me, I'd recommend taking electrolytes - whether in tab or powder form, as they're excellent at maintaining your hydration levels and optimum fluid balance.

Fitness & Training

My training started in the middle of February 2019, before I fell off track by the end of the month. For some reason, I didn't do anything in March. But as April came around, I thought I'd best get out and put in some miles. I didn't have a dedicated training plan as such; the idea was just to get out often and as much as possible. I had set my sights on completing end to end in August, surely that would be enough time to get to a reasonable fitness? I thought.

My fitness at the time was probably around average. I no longer had a car, so my commute to work included a 2-mile walk each day involving a very steep hill, a round trip equating to 4 miles. Over several months, walking every day had such a positive effect on my fitness levels. So much so, that I was astonished how much it benefitted me.

In total, through February to July, I completed 25 training rides, not very many at all, thinking about it. It mainly consisted of one ride of around 27 miles (45km) during the weekday evenings, along with a longer ride of about 49-62 miles (80-100 km) at the weekend. The lengthiest trip that formed part of my training was a journey from Bristol and back to Exeter at 86 miles (140 km).

One mistake I made during my preparations was not having done any practice rides with my bike fully laden. The day I cycled down to the train station to board the train to London was the first time I had ridden with all my equipment attached. So, it's worthwhile ensuring that you do a few practice runs to make sure you're comfortable and everything is working correctly.

However, as I found out when riding JOGLE, turning the pedals was relatively easy. The real battle is with the mind - the ability to wake up every morning and carry on covering the miles whether you're in pain, feeling exhausted, having to contend with poor weather conditions, or otherwise.

Costs

Costs for undertaking the End to End challenge can range from hundreds to the thousands. It all depends on what equipment you have already, and how long you'd like to spend completing the route. For me, the costs were, in the end, very high. I had a lot of the gear already, so adding up everything I needed to buy plus the costs of food and accommodation then it probably came in at between £1500 - £2000.

As soon as I decided to embark on cycling end to end at the start of 2019, I started to purchase the items I did need and booking accommodation over several months to spread the costs.

I did try to limit my expenditure by wild camping several nights. However, despite the costs, I saw the trip as a once in a lifetime opportunity, an unforgettable experience; so it was more than worth it.

I have broken down my expenditure into sections to provide an overview. For full disclosure, I've only included items I needed to purchase and not what I owned already. More information on everything I took can be found under Kit List & Equipment on page 16.

Bike Extras

Hopefully, you have a bicycle already. I ended up using my old mountain bike, which I originally paid £600 for back in 2012. I upgraded a few bits and ensured it was in top condition by taking it in for a thorough service beforehand. If you don't own a bicycle, think long term before you go and purchase the first one that you see. Will you be using it after the tour?

Touring Tyres	£60.00
Full Service	£50.00
Padded Seat Cover	£17.00
Ergonomic Grips	£15.00
Estimated Cost:	**£142.00**

Travel

Costs of getting to the start and leaving the endpoint will vary depending on where you live in the country and how you decide to travel. To try and keep costs low, take the time to have a good look around and try out different combinations of travel to weigh up all your options. Also, book your travel tickets as far in advance as possible. Train prices are a lot cheaper three months in advance, which is worth bearing in mind.

Exeter St David's to Paddington	£20.00
London Euston to Inverness	£50.00
Inverness to Wick	£8.00
Penzance to Exeter St David's	£20.00
Estimated Cost:	**£100.00**

Bike Packing Panniers and Bags

This was another significant expense, although it doesn't have to be. There are many decent brands out there who make touring bags; you just need to shop around for the best deals. In the end, I went for one of the more expensive brands as their products are extremely popular with the bike packing community. As I have found out when buying outdoor gear in the past, I prefer to spend money on decent equipment that is going to last.

Saddle pack	£132.00
Handlebar Pack	£104.00
Top Tube Pack	£26.00
Frame pack	£66.00
Accessory Pack	£50.00
Estimated Cost:	**£378.00**

Equipment

I already had a lot of the equipment, especially tools to maintain my bike. But here are some of the extra items that I picked up. These included a few little extras for my camera.

Spare Tubes	£12.00
Midge spray/face net	£12.00
Krypto Lock Flex	£10.00
Spork	£5.00
Water Bottles x2	£18.00
Pocket Trowel	£3.00
Camera Mount	£15.00
SD Card	£26.00
Roll Mat	£45.00
Estimated Cost:	**£146.00**

Cycle Clothing

Since you're going to be spending an awful lot of time in the saddle, suitable clothing is essential to keep you comfortable and protect you from the elements. British weather is notoriously unpredictable, so you'll no doubt encounter poor weather conditions at some point.

The figure below is an estimate of how much extra clothing I needed to buy. A good source for cheap cycle clothing is Decathlon and Wiggle's own-brand DHB; these are great options if you have a smaller budget.

Gloves	£20.00
Cycling Jersey	£80.00
Bib Shorts	£100.00
Fleece	£90.00
Waterproof Bottoms	£10.00
Aqua Shoes	£20.00
Estimated Cost:	**£320.00**

Food

Another significant expense, but you shouldn't skimp on food and drink. This was a hard one for me to track as I was buying all sorts. This included stopping at shops and cafes along the way. Not to mention trolley dashes at supermarkets on some evenings!

Another example is having a large evening meal, including drinks at a pub or hotel. This is likely to set you back around £25 a pop. That's not including breakfast which will likely be an additional cost unless included in the price of your stay. Times that by ten days and it equates to £250, which doesn't even include snacks for the day.

Even if you decide to go to the supermarket to pick up supplies, which I did multiple times, I ended up spending around the same amount of money.

The combined cost of food: -

Cafes/shops/Supermarkets/B&Bs

Estimated Cost: **£300.00 - £400.00**

Accommodation

Below is all my accommodation expenditure for the nights I did stay in pre-booked accommodation and campsites. The Crask Inn is a unique place, so I didn't mind the extra outlay to spend the night at Britain's remotest pub. At all the places I stayed at, I was warmly welcomed and had a fantastic stay.

Thurso Camp Site	£10.00
Crask Inn	£60.00
Aviemore Hostel	£27.00
Pitlochry Hostel	£20.00
New Lanark Hostel	£25.00
Westlands Country Park	£10.00
Manchester Premier Inn	£41.00
The Croft Bridgnorth	£40.00
Mendip Camp	£8.00
Estimated Cost:	**£241.00**

Getting to the start or leaving the endpoint.

As I wanted to keep travel costs as low as possible, taking the train was the cheapest option for me. When I first researched train fares, a direct train from Exeter to Inverness with onward travel to Wick came in at around £259. After a bit of searching, I found a much cheaper alternative. However, it would increase my travel time a great deal, from stepping out my door to arriving at John O'Groats took me near enough 24 hours. But since it saved me a considerable sum of money, it was worth it.

My travel plans involved getting a weekday afternoon train from Exeter to Paddington, costing around £20. It would then be a 12-hour train ride from London Euston to Inverness on the overnight sleeper at £50. Finally, the train up to Wick costing £8. Altogether, the entire trip came to around £80; a fantastic deal I thought, to get from one side of the country to the other.

Leaving Penzance to get back to Exeter was a late weekday train. I didn't pre-book this train, or make a bicycle reservation, as I wasn't sure what time I would make it back to the station. The train was practically empty and cost around £20. Depending on your budget and which way you'd like to cycle end to end, there are several options to get to and from both places.

By Train

The preferred option is going to by rail and will likely be the cheapest. Fortunately, you'll find a train station in reasonably close proximity to either the start or finish point. For example, John O'Groats is 16 miles from Wick, and Land's End is roughly 12 miles from Penzance. So, be sure to account for the extra distance you will need to cover on starting or leaving.

You will likely have to get multiple trains on your journey. To get to Wick, you'll need to take a train from Inverness which involves a journey time of around 4.5 hours. Penzance is easier to get to as it is the last stop on the main trunk line of services running between London or services running to the North on through to Edinburgh, where you'll need to change services again to get to Inverness.

For any train journey that you undertake, ensure that you arrange a reservation for your bicycle to avoid any potential disappointment that will arise if you're not allowed to board the service with your bike. Thankfully, it's easy to do this at the same time when booking your tickets on the respective company's website.

An important point to mention, make sure to reserve a bicycle space on the service between Wick/Inverness and ensure you book as far in advanced as possible. During the peak summer months, demand is high, and spaces fill up extremely quickly. More often than not, there is only room for four bicycles. Plus, reservations are checked by the train guard before boarding.

Cycling between Wick and John O'Groats, it is merely the case of following the A99. The A30 is the main road running between Land's End and Penzance. Just be aware this road tends to get very busy, especially during the summer months. It might be advisable to head along the quieter road such as the B3315, running south along the peninsula. Both routes should take under an hour to cycle.

You will find several useful rail services listed below: -

Trainline
www.thetrainline.com

Scot Rail
www.scotrail.co.uk

Cross Country
www.crosscountrytrains.co.uk

GWR
www.gwr.com

By Plane

If you don't want to endure a long and tiring train journey or you're coming from abroad, Inverness Airport is a great option. This is because it provides connections with many cities around the UK, including Bristol, Birmingham, London, Manchester, along with Jersey and several cities throughout Europe.

Likewise, at the other end of the country in Cornwall is Newquay's airport which is the closest commercial airport to Land's End serving London, Newcastle, Edinburgh, Glasgow, Aberdeen as well as a few cities throughout Europe. Onward travel can then be made by train from Newquay to St Austell where you'll need to make a connection to Penzance.

Flight times to Newquay

London: 1 hr 09 min

Newcastle: 1 hr 15 min

Edinburgh: 3 hr 50 min

Glasgow: 2 hr 40 min

Aberdeen: 3 hr 5 min

Flight times to Inverness

Manchester: 1 hr 15 min

Birmingham: 1 hr 30 min

Bristol: 1 hr 25 min

London: 1 hr 45 mi

Be aware that taking a bicycle on as luggage does present problems with the amount of weight that you're typically allowed. With all your equipment, it's likely to bump up the price considerably. Also, you'd want to be safe in the knowledge that your bike is going to survive the journey. So, it's advisable to pack your bicycle in a sturdy bike box. But don't forget to consider what you would do with the bike box at the other end!

Visit the following links to find out more information about flights: -

Newquay Airport
www.invernessairport.co.uk

Inverness Airport
www.cornwallairportnewquay.com

By Taxi

Another way of getting to/from John O'Groats and Inverness is by using the John O'Groats Bike Transport taxi service - dedicated to providing transport between the two points. Just be aware that if you're travelling alone, this option does come at a premium. Therefore, it is best to check the dates on their website to see when others are making the trip so that you can split the cost. If there are a few of you going, prices start from £60.

They do also provide a courier service as an alternative, which involves packing up your bike and ship to your home address if you didn't want the inconvenience of making your way back home with your bicycle. They can even transport bicycles to the start point waiting for you at John O'Groats if you decide to do JOGLE.

Find out more information by visiting their website below.

www.johnogroatsbiketransport.co.uk

JOGLE/LEJOG Facilities

Both complexes have facilities if you'd like to enjoy a bite to eat and a coffee, do some souvenir shopping, or are searching for accommodation. John O'Groats is a little bit disappointing, but you're probably not going to be there for very long, so it doesn't matter all that much. In 2010, it did receive a reward for being "Scotland's most dismal town". However, in recent years, redevelopment work has been carried out and has since become a trendy tourist spot.

Land's End is the more enjoyable of the two locations, all thanks to its extensive complex of shops, eateries, and attractions for families. Twice a week in August, they even have fireworks displays. Also, when you're at Land's End, don't forget to sign the visitors' book in the lobby of The Land's End Hotel, a book of everyone who has set off or completed End to End.

EQUIPMENT & KIT LIST

What Kind of Bicycle do I Need?

A bike is an essential bit of kit you're going to need. But what kind of bike is suitable? Well, you can choose any type you want, as long as it is roadworthy and safe to use. There have been some beautiful and exciting ways people have completed End to End, unicycles, penny farthings, and Bromptons - to name but a few. You certainly don't need to spend a lot of money on an expensive and fancy aero bike.

Even though I had a road bike, I decided to put my old mountain bike to good use. My 2011 Specialized Rockhopper had been gathering dust in the garage for quite a few years. Because of the gearing, the chainset being 22/32/44T with a nine-speed 11-34 cassette, I thought it would make things a bit easier getting up and over the hills, especially being fully laden. Even when I bought it all those years ago, I probably never made much use of it. However, it certainly holds a lot of sentimental value to me now.

As I'd not used the bike had not in years, a few parts needed changing. So, I replaced the grips, bent rear derailleur, the chain, and I also swapped out the knobbly tyres for touring tyres, which were extra puncture resistant. Finally, to ensure that it was in top condition, I also ensured I got it in for a full service a few weeks before.

My 2011 Specialized Rockhopper

Once I'd gotten the maintenance out of the way, the next step was deciding on the type of bag setup I would be using. In the end, I went for the fresh bike packing look, rather than using the more traditional touring panniers.

Then, I set about creating a list of all the equipment I would need. The best way I found was to create a spreadsheet, like the one below, and create headings for each category. Underneath each grouping, I then wrote a list of all the items that it would need.

Item	Shop	Price	Acquired
Personal			
Helmet	-	-	✓
Fluorescent jacket	-	-	✓
Cycling Jersey x2	-	-	✓
Cycling Shorts x2	-	-	✓
Sunglasses	-	-	✓
...			
Bicycle Equipment			
Saddle Bag	Apidura	£132.00	✓
Handlebar Bag	Apidura	£104.00	
Top Bar Bag	Amazon	£26.00	
...			

Example of spreadsheet

Inevitably over time, the list grew an awful lot. Even on the day that I was due to set off, I found myself remembering to pick up other bits and pieces that might come in useful, little things like tape, extra rags, toilet tissue, the kitchen sink! It eventually got to a point where I could have gone on and on - squeezing more into every nook and cranny of my already bulging bags. The whole idea, to begin with, was to pack as light as possible. But I soon realised that I just had to say enough! I could always pick items up en-route if needed, as my bike already weighed an absolute ton!

I managed to squeeze all of my equipment into four bike packing bags, a 17L saddle bag, 3L frame bag, 14L handlebar bag, and a 1L top tube bag. Plus, I took a 10L trail running backpack. Now, I'm certainly not paid by Apidura to promote their products. But, Apidura straight away caught my eye when initially looking into which bike packing bags to purchase. They came across as a very professional company, with their products being well tested and hugely popular within the bike packing community. So, I didn't hesitate in purchasing some of their products.

Although one of the more expensive brands, they do a range of bags in different price scales. If you'd like to find out more about them, then you'll find plenty of useful information at the back of the book. For me, it was between the Expedition Series (Waterproof), or the Backcountry Series (Weatherproof).

From my past experiences of the Scottish climate, the bags storing my clothes and sleeping system would definitely need to be waterproof! For that reason, I decided to purchase the Expedition Series (waterproof) saddlebag and handlebar pack. The frame pack would be the 3-litre Backcountry Pack, which would hold tools, spare parts, and items that didn't matter if they got wet. I made an exception to the top tube pack, opting for the Topeak Toploader bag at only £26.00, a fraction of what Apidura charge, and a fantastic choice indeed.

Little did I know that I would experience eight days of near enough torrential rain. It's for that very reason I must say that I was glad to have paid a bit extra to get higher-quality items for my trip. The waterproof bags, in particular, stood up fantastically in the awful weather I endured coming down through Scotland. In my experience, I find that when waterproof material becomes fully saturated, it eventually seeps through. Thankfully, this wasn't the case on my adventure, with everything remaining completely dry throughout.

Below you'll find an overview of the kit that I took with me. I packed light so it gives you some idea on the bare minimum of what you might want to take. I split everything into each pack as follows, which I found worked great in my experience.

On Person

Below are all the items I wore. An important point to mention is having a fluorescent jacket. A few of the days, especially when passing down through Scotland, the visibility was poor with rain and mist. Even though I had lights, the jacket gave me a lot more visibility so I would be easier to spot by motorists. I also decided against going for clipless pedals, for a greater range of movement, preferring to wear my trainers. These would certainly allow me to walk around a lot easier.

- Fluorescent Jacket
- Long Bib Shorts
- Socks
- Helmet
- Base Layer Top
- Cycling Jersey
- Trail Running Shoes
- Cycling Cap

Trail Running Pack

My Salomon trail running pack was a godsend. I bought it some years prior, as trail running is another favourite pastime of mine. It came with a 1.5-litre water bladder, so it doubled up as an additional water bottle.

As it only has a 10-litre capacity, I used it to carry essentials I needed to hand, including waterproofs which came out more than anything else! It's also where I kept my Sustrans Land's End to John O'Groats guidebook when raining, my GoPro, spare emergency bags of sweets, and any other food that I could cram in.

- ☐ GoPro
- ☐ Bags of Sweets
- ☐ Water Proof Jacket
- ☐ Notebook and Pen
- ☐ Power Bank
- ☐ Water Proof Trousers

Salomon Trail Running Pack (10l)

Top Tube Bag

The Topeak Toploader bag was an absolute bargain, and far cheaper than the alternative from Apidura. With a 0.75 litre capacity, it was perfect for storing easy-access food. I used it for small valuable items such as keys, my wallet, along with a spare battery for my GoPro. I also managed to squeeze in my battery charger supply for powering my phone when I was using it as a satnav. And of course, a few cereal bars in there as well, for good measure.

The Toploader bag attaches using three nylon straps, with two securing the pack to the top tube, alongside another at the front which loops around the stem. A bonus is that it comes with an integrated waterproof cover - safely secured in a hidden side pocket.

- ☐ Cereal Bars
- ☐ Lighter
- ☐ Spare Phone
- ☐ Keys
- ☐ Wallet
- ☐ Power Bank/GoPro Charger

Topeak Toploader Bag (0.75l)

Handlebar Pack

As I would be wild camping, the pack holding my sleeping bag needed to be waterproof, as there was no way I could afford for it to get wet. The largest waterproof handlebar pack was 14 litres, which ended up being a perfect fit, so naturally, I decided this would be ideal for holding my sleeping system setup. That, along with the gear that I would only need when I arrived at my destination.

I've always preferred camping using a tarp, as it's lightweight, can be set up in seconds, takes up little space, and you can see what's going on around you during daylight hours.

The pack has three securing points, two straps which attach to the handlebars, while a third wraps around the top of the forks. But most of the time, I forgot about this one.

Apidura Expedition Series (14l)

- ☐ Sleeping Bag
- ☐ Tarpaulin
- ☐ Trowel
  (In case I got caught short)

- ☐ Roll Mat
- ☐ Beanie Hat
- ☐ Toiletry Bag
  - ▪ Toothbrush
  - ▪ Toothpaste
  - ▪ Shower Gel
  - ▪ Hand Wipes

Accessory Pack

The accessory pack was a last-minute purchase for me. The reason for me buying it is so that I could easily carry the food and supplies I bought during my preparations. The pack clips to the front of the handlebar pack and supplements it as opposed to being a standalone bag, so it's great for storing any essentials that you may have. Since all my packs were full, I had nowhere for a lot of it to go. So I'm glad I decided to bite the bullet on this one in the end.

It was a great addition as it meant I could keep most of my main meals and other snacks in one easily accessible place. I used it to store bags of rice, tuna, along with cereal bars and bags of trail mix.

Apidura Expedition Series (4.5l)

<table>
<tr><td>☐ Packets of Boiled Rice</td><td>☐ Packets of Tuna</td></tr>
<tr><td>☐ Lots of Cereal Bars</td><td>☐ Bags of Trail Mix</td></tr>
</table>

Saddle Pack

The saddlebag was the most expensive of all the packs that I bought. But like the handlebar pack, it needed to be waterproof as it would hold all my clothes and the numerous electrical wires I needed to charge my devices. At 17 litres, the pack is somewhat limiting in terms of space. I didn't get to do any washing on my trip until I reached Gloucester. So, it was inevitable that the bag would get a bit smelly from the sweaty socks!

The pack has three attachment points, with two large straps wrap around the seat post, alongside another for securing it around the saddle bars. There was no specific way of packing apart from ramming everything in and pulling it tight, saving the bag of electrical cables last in case I needed quick access to them. The top of the pack also has elastic securing straps, which I found to be extremely useful. This is where I had a supermarket bag secured full of food for most of the trip.

Apidura Expedition Series (17l)

- Fleece
- Base Layer Trousers
- Short Bib Shorts
- Flip Flops
- Cooking System
- Electrical Cables

- Base Layer Tops x2
- Cycling Jersey
- Shorts
- Travel Towel
- Socks x4

Frame Pack

Ideally, I would have liked to have had the complete matching set of packs, just to satisfy my mild OCD. However, I settled on the backcountry frame pack, as it was much cheaper than the waterproof version. Here, I kept all the gear which didn't matter if it got wet such as tools, oil, cable ties, and spare parts. Not to mention all the extra cereal bars that I could stuff in!

The backcountry frame pack attached at three points – two of which were along the top tube, and one on the down tube. Although not waterproof, they are weatherproof and very durable, so could handle a little drizzle.

Since Apidura caters for many frame sizes, they do provide A4 pack templates which you can print from their site. Once printed, you tape them together, cut around the outline, then match them to your bike to see the best fit. Due to the small frame of my bicycle, the 3-litre compact version fitted perfectly.

Apidura Backcountry Series (3l)

- ☐ Tubes x2
- ☐ Cable Ties
- ☐ Multi-Tool
- ☐ Chain Tool
- ☐ Spare Chain Links
- ☐ Tent Pegs
- ☐ Hand Pumps
- ☐ Fire Lighters (never got around to making a fire)

- ☐ Spork
- ☐ Puncture Repair Kit
- ☐ Insulation Tape
- ☐ Midge Face Net
- ☐ Chain Lube
- ☐ Cleaning Rags x2
- ☐ Tyre Levers

MY JOURNAL

Day 00
Exeter to John O'Groats - 677 mi (1,089 km)

The day had finally arrived! After all the months of planning, dreaming, and buying gear for completing John O'Groats to Land's End, the day was here. Although, it has to be said, getting to the start was the part I was not looking forward to the most.

The morning started relatively relaxed, - enjoying a catch up with my friend, picking up some final bits, and making some last-minute preparations to my kit. With everything prepped by around mid-afternoon, I set off to catch the 15:39 train from Exeter St David's to London Paddington.

A slight oversight, I thought, but riding down to the station was the first time I had ridden my bike with all my gear attached - a schoolboy error if I do say so myself. I should have taken it for an extended test run beforehand to see if there would be any issues with straps and cables, although they do say that hindsight is a wonderful thing!

Waiting on the platform in zone 2 (where the bicycle carriage was due to stop) a sudden feeling of apprehension came over me. Did I fully know what I was letting myself in for? I asked myself. Before this point, I had watched countless touring videos, read numerous blogs, and more to prepare myself mentally. If worse came to worse, I could purchase whatever I needed along the way. But I had never undertaken anything like this before. Would I be able to complete it? Well, if I immediately dismissed the negative thoughts, of course, I would!

The train pulled up, the doors opened, and to my surprise, there were no cycle spaces! This was the wrong carriage, and the screen had lied to me! To make matters worse, there were no signs on the outside, indicating where the cycle spaces were. With the panic quickly setting in, I frantically jogged back down the train peering in door after door, conscious that any second the whistle would blow, and doors would start to close. After all, not many people got on given that it was mid-afternoon on a Wednesday.

To my relief, I finally spotted the cycle hangers. It was at this point; I used all my strength to haul my bike onto the train (with some difficulty, might I add!). It weighed a ton, but luckily, I managed to heave the front wheel up to secure it in the hook before taking a seat and settling in for the 2.5-hour journey to London.

I didn't know it at the time, but during my struggle attaching the front wheel to the hooks, I managed to take a gouge of rubber out of the tyre, and I didn't notice until I got to Inverness. Luckily, it didn't go all the way through to the inner tube or provide any problems throughout the cycle tour.

Upon arriving at London Paddington, it was a 2-mile ride across London to Euston Station. I must admit that riding through a major city is a new experience for me, and so I wasn't sure what to expect. Thankfully, I discovered that it wasn't all that bad, mostly down to the fact I missed the rush hour chaos. One thing that immediately stood out was the amount people whizzing about on Brompton bicycles – something I hadn't seen all that much before this point.

After safely making it to Euston, I had about two and a half hours to kill. I decided to take a walk around to the front of the station and take some pictures for the blog, but scaffolding and building sites surrounded the area, along with large crowds of people - I couldn't believe how busy it was!

As I stood looking at Google Maps, I was greeted by a fellow who I would politely describe as a down and out. He complimented me on my bicycle and asked if he could have a go; I declined by telling him I had a train to catch, quickly making my way inside the station before any potential trouble arose. It was the busiest station I had ever seen, with hundreds of people staring at information boards waiting for their trains to arrive. I made my way over to an empty wall where I propped myself up against it, spending the remaining two hours people watching.

Finally, the announcement came over the speaker "the Caledonian sleeper to Inverness is ready to board on platform 1". Thank God! I made my way over to the waiting train, quickly loaded my bike and found my seat in the carriage. I wanted to keep the price as low as possible so had chosen the cheap seats at £50. Initially, I booked a place on the new fleet, which was supposed to be entering service. However, with a delay in rolling out the brand-new carriages, this meant travelling on the extremely dated train, probably built in the 70-80s.

On finding my seat and to my horror, there were no power sockets to charge anything. I wouldn't be able to use my phone for entertainment, so naturally, I had to turn it off for the entire journey to conserve the battery. Almost immediately, I thought this would lead to getting lost in my thoughts and getting little to no sleep for the whole 12-hour trip.

Luckily, I found the wide laid-back chairs to be quite comfy, allowing me to get settled rathe. Pleased that everything had gone so smoothly thus far, I was now bound for Scotland. A bonus is that I even got about 3 hours' sleep along the way!

After I arrived at Inverness station, I spotted two other cyclists with fully loaded bikes. They probably had double the amount of gear I had. Each had four panniers, two front and back, along with a massive dry bag strapped across the back two. I did wonder if they had completed LEJOG and how on earth it would be possible to ride with all that gear.

It was yet another couple of hours wait for the last train to Wick. So, I decided to stroll past many occupied benches before stumbling upon another empty wall that I could prop myself up against. Only this time, I was sitting, reminiscing on the other times that I had visited Inverness, and thinking to myself that I would be passing back through in a few days.

Eventually, the display board flickered into life, displaying the platform of the train to Wick. I once again, excitedly, scurried over to the platform to the waiting train. I had my bicycle reservation checked off before climbing on board for the final section of my train journey, which would take four and a half hours. This last part was probably the worst out of the lot because it seemed to take an eternity. At this point, all I wanted was to get underway. But at the same time, I was intrigued as I was venturing into uncharted territory. I had never been further north than Inverness before, and I had plenty of beautiful scenery to captivate me along the way.

As I mentioned under the travelling to the start or leaving the endpoint section if you plan on taking your bike on the train which runs between Wick and Inverness, ensure that you have booked a bicycle reservation in advance. After all, there are only four spaces on offer, with demand being high during the spring/ summer months - mostly from people returning from LEJOG.

Day 01
John O'Groats to Thurso - 21.39 mi (34.42 km)

I arrived at Wick just after 3:00 pm as there was a slight delay in the journey time. The exhausting experience of what I thought was a monumental journey, vanished from thought. John O'Groats, the starting point, seemed like it was

John O'Groats, the starting point

just around the corner. But there was still 16 miles to cover before I could reach the famous signpost and begin my journey home. Again, I made final preparations to my bike, securing lights, tightening straps, changing into my riding gear, and setting directions on Google Maps. Then, I was ready to go and went on my way.

It is a straightforward route to follow to get to John O'Groats. All you need to do is head left out of the station, over the bridge, and stay on the A99 to John O'Groats. I was expecting the worse with regards to the weather conditions, as I can imagine the northernmost point must get battered by the strong North Sea winds. But, to my surprise, it wasn't bad. And despite a dull atmosphere and grey tone to the bleak landscape, the sky was overcast with glimpses of blue sky in the distance.

The route seemed reasonably flat, until reaching Freswick. Here, a long gradual incline led up and passed through a vast expanse of moorland either side of the A99, before the final descent into John O'Groats - the northernmost point of mainland Britain. The closer I got, the more excited I felt.

After rounding the final corner, it was a long straight that leads down to the iconic area, which I could see in the distance. Now, I had a massive smile on my face, full of happiness. I was happy to reach the most northern point of mainland Britain, more so because it's an area that I had never seen before. One day, I would very much like to go back and visit.

Looking at my watch, it had taken near enough 24 hours from stepping out my front door back in Exeter. As I pulled up close to the shops, I quickly looked around for the famous signpost so I could get my picture taken; I spotted it and headed straight over. A couple who just completed LEJOG were in the middle of taking pictures, both turning to congratulate me on also arriving, thinking I had just finished. But it was the opposite – my adventure had only just begun!

Another guy had also just arrived to finish his LEJOG, who I believe was called Steve. I obliged in taking his picture standing in front of the signpost, and he returned the favour. After informing me that he had completed LEJOG in nine days, I was eager to find out more. We continued chatting and went into the café where he very kindly bought me a coffee. I was so intrigued by his story, and Steve was happy to share the details so I'd know more about what I was letting myself in for. It turns out that he had endured terrible weather and cycled along some parts of the A9. A mad man, I thought. I was in complete astonishment!

With the final sip of my coffee, I decided I couldn't hang around too long as time was getting on. I had another 15 miles to cover before reaching my first night's stop at Thurso Bay Caravan & Camping Park, a campsite situated on the coast of Thurso. So, I thanked Steve for the coffee, congratulated him once again, and headed outside.

I had a quick look around the area - taking a few pictures and buying a customary magnet and postcards to send home to family members. At one point, I was even greeted by a Danish naval officer waiting for his ship to come in. He approached me and enquired what I was doing, after which we chatted for a bit. After a long while, I politely excused myself, as the time had finally come to set off for home.

After a tightening of straps, I set off up the road from which I whizzed down with much excitement, making a right turn at the sign directing me to Thurso, some 15 miles away. As I was following the Sustrans Cycle Network, it was mainly quiet roads that I would be following. So, rather than continue along the A836 to Thurso, I opted for a quiet road to Castletown. Along the way, I stopped to admire the long sweeping beach and remarked what a lovely place it would be to wild camp.

After passing through the village and stopping off at the local shop for some much-needed water, I again kept to the back road NCN Route 1, which eventually joined up with the final section of the A9 leading into Thurso. In all, my experience so far had been rather pleasant, despite the lack of sleep. A bonus was that the weather wasn't bad at all.

I arrived at Thurso's campsite sometime just after 7:00 pm. But it wasn't long before I came across my first problem. Using a tarp to camp does present a problem, as you usually need to tie at least two ends to something to create some sort of lean-to shelter. Looking around, all I could find was the lamp post that stood on a public path which went around the perimeter of the campsite. I propped my bike up against the tone fence and tied one end of the tarp to the lamp post, draped it over my bike so that it was fully covered, and pegged the other corners into the ground; it was enough to keep me dry at least. It didn't even occur to me at the time, but the light from the lamp post would be shining right above me for the entire night!

Once I had set up camp, I sat against the fence, sheltered from the wind, cooked up some rice and tuna for dinner, pleased in the knowledge that I was finally underway, heading back in the direction of home. Soon after, I crawled into my sleeping bag in an attempt to get some much-needed rest. And even though I spent most of the night tossing and turning, I managed to get a few hours' sleep, at least.

Day 02
Thurso to Crask - 67.34 mi (108.37 km)

I woke early from the 2-3 hours' sleep I had managed to get and decided I should set off early to take advantage of the quiet roads. After a quick wash, I packed up all my gear which seemed to take more time than it should have from all the fussing about I had to do. I

Leaving Thurso

secured my bags and headed out of the campsite continuing on NCN Route 1, along the B874. It was surprisingly busy considering the number of trucks that came hurtling past. The road eventually joined back up with the A836, and I stayed on here for roughly 20 miles until I reached Bettyhill. The A836 was quite a lovely cycle, as it's pretty quiet for an A road. Mainly used by tourists, it features plenty of long gradual inclines which made for equally long descents.

Passing through the village of Bettyhill, I immediately spotted the general store. I thought this would be an excellent place to stop off and fuel up. I dashed in to pick up some Scotch pies, chocolate bars, and a couple of cans of pop. I headed around the corner and parked up at a picnic table beside the local park, managing to scoff the lot within minutes, just as it started spitting rain. Little did I know, that these first signs of light rain would be the start of near enough eight days of torrential downpours and getting saturated each day.

Leaving Bettyhill, it was another 12 miles to Tongue. I don't remember much of it, other than the rain which had started lashing down. But now wasn't the time for complaining, it was a case of keeping my head down and getting on with it. I donned my waterproofs which didn't stand a chance, with only a pair of sunglasses preventing my face getting covered in spray. The problem was that I could hardly see a thing from the brown tint, but they did keep the water out of my eyes.

After seeing the entrance for Weavers Craft Shop & Café, I didn't need to think twice; I was straight in there. Thoroughly wet through, I took great delight in ordering a toastie, cake, and coffee savouring the warmth and seeking refuge from the rain.

But it was no use in putting it off any longer; I needed to press on. So, put on my wet jacket, stepped out into the pouring rain, and continued on my way. After rounding the corner from leaving the café, I branched left, staying on the A836. It was at this point that I had a huge phycological boost, I was no longer heading along the top of Scotland, I had started to head down the country, which meant every pedal and every mile was getting me closer to home and the finish line.

Although it was straight into an incline leading up above the village of Tongue, I did stop to take in the sweeping panoramic view of the Kyle of Tongue. In the distance, I could see Castle Bharrich perched high on the rugged hillside over to the left, with the causeway to the right. Although the view was hampered by the mist and rain, on a clear day, it would be spectacular, I thought to myself.

After reaching the top, it was about a 2-mile descent to the edge of Loch Loyal. With the rain still pouring, I continued along close to the side of the loch, having to pull into the passing places every so often to let cars pass me. The distance from both ends of Loch Loyal was only just over 4 miles, although it certainly seemed longer than that.

At the bottom left corner of Loch Loyal, the road continued for a short distance before turning left and heading over the river that joins Loch Coulside. And when on the other side of the bank, I discovered a Scottish Bothy, so I decided to take a few minutes recess, a welcome break from the weather. But thinking back, I'm not entirely sure it was an official bothy.

Leaving the bothy was another long steady incline. Coming over the brow of the hill and starting the descent, I could see buildings in the far distance and a thought popped into my head, was it the Crask Inn? I instantly shooed the thoughts away as I didn't want to get my hopes up. Regardless, I gave the map a quick check anyway, only to discover that it was Altnaharra; with another 7 miles still to go before I reached The Crask Inn.

When I eventually did see Crask, I proudly gave a triumphant shout, with my morale returning at the speed of light! A warm bed for the night, a three-course meal, and a chance to sit down and relax with a pint. To top it all of, I was finally able to get out of the rain and dry off.

Entering Britain's remotest pub, a group of around sixteen cyclists greeted me. My first thoughts were, where did everyone come from? Surely this group can't be staying here tonight? But as it turned out,

A pint and wee dram at The Crask Inn

a supported group of riders had just finished their second to last leg at the Crask Inn. They were due to return the next day and complete their final leg of LEJOG. Thankfully they weren't staying long, with a bus scheduled to pick them up soon. Phew, I thought, as I was keen to sit down and relax in peace.

I ordered myself a well-deserved pint and dram of whiskey from the Crask's vast selection and chatted to a few of the friendly cyclists, who were shocked to discover that I was riding north to south, part wild camping on the route. One of the group was named Claire. Claire, if you're reading this, thank you for taking the time to email me asking how I was getting on. It was a much-needed morale boost, on my arrival to Bridgnorth on Day 12.

After the group had left, I stored my bike away and was given the keys to my room. I finally managed to get out of my wet gear, hanging it above the roaring open fire in the bar. I then decided to make the most of the drinks on offer and enjoy another pint. In total, there were seven of us staying for the night; two other cyclists, a Scottish couple who had decided on escaping the Edinburgh Fringe Festival, and a German couple over on holiday.

One of the nice things about dinner is that the staff encourage all guests to sit around the same table and socialise with each other, which I thought was a great idea. The home cooked food was terrific. It included a starter, fish pie for the main, and a dessert to finish. It didn't take long for me to devour this. So next, I returned to the bar for another pint.

All in all, my recommendation is that if you ever decide to do LEJOG/JOGLE, you need to plan in a night at The Crask Inn. It's a unique little place, famed for being Britain's remotest pub; with its staff members being extremely accommodating and friendly.

Day 03
The Crask Inn to Inverness - 72.16 mi (116.13 km)

After enjoying my evening meal and socialising at the bar, I eventually called it a night and got my head down. But before I knew it, I was awake again! Although I did have the best night's sleep since I had left Exeter. So, it was certainly worth staying here at The Crask Inn. I went down for breakfast at 7:30 am and fuelled up on as much food as possible. I got started with some porridge, which happened to be one of the most delicious bowls that I've ever had. Shortly after, I enjoyed a fry up, toast, and about 3 cups of coffee. All in all, this set me up perfectly for the ride down to Inverness.

As soon as I stepped outside, it didn't take long for the midges to attack! When planning my trip, I wasn't sure what to expect and how bad they would be. Fortunately, this was my only experience with them, and it was short-lived. A squirt of repellent on my hands and face, and I was good to go.

Just as I was strapping on my bags and carrying out final checks, the large cycling group from the evening before returned to the Crask Inn to finish their final leg to John O'Groats. After saying hello and wishing them well, I then continued on my way down the A836, heading in the opposite direction to Lairg. This stretch was, for the most part, all downhill - making it a gentle, relaxed start to the day during which I quickly covered 12 miles while hardly breaking a sweat.

On reaching Lairg, I pulled into the large car park overlooking Little Loch Shin, a manmade loch that was created by the hydroelectric dam scheme. Here, I grabbed a quick break, pleased for getting here reasonably quickly. And what better way to treat myself than by indulging in a celebratory bag of Haribo!

Once I'd left the car park, I then headed over the bridge onto the A839. Shortly after, I headed along the B864 - the road which winds along the side of the valley, running parallel with the River Shin. Most of this section was encapsulated by woodland either side, with glimpses of the river flowing fast below. But to my surprise, out of nowhere, a hidden gem appeared - the Falls of Shin Visitor Attraction. Even the café happened to catch my eye, despite my hearty breakfast! I went in for a closer inspection, but I decided against stopping in the end. It felt like I was still early into the ride, and I wanted to make up some distance. But at a later date, I discovered that it is famous for being one of the best places in Scotland to watch wild salmon leaping upstream.

After my quick recce of the café, I continued on my way. Riding down the A386 into Bonar Bridge, I stopped briefly for a few quick photos and to look at the map. After this, it was then time to head over the bridge and around into Ardgay. On spotting Ardgay Shop and Highland Café, this time I felt obliged to sample a coffee and cake - a treat for doing so well, I thought. It was also an excellent time to stock up on supplies of Haribo and a couple of cans of pop for later on.

After a 30-minute rest, it was time to press on. So, I continued along the NCN Route before turning left on the B9176. I knew what was coming, and I had already prepped myself mentally. As soon as I turned right onto the B9176, it was straight into what would be a 2-mile climb. I quickly found the easiest gear and settled into the climb at a snail's pace; no doubt walking would have been quicker! It would be much like climbing up and over a mountain. Or, at least in between two - Struie and Cnoc an Liath-bhaid.

At this point, the weather was on my side. It held out for most of the day, but just as I had passed the Struie Hill Viewpoint, a light rain started to descend on me. It wasn't a lot, but, I still decided to pull over and put on my waterproofs, which always seemed like a time-consuming process; even more so when it came to taking them off.

From my experience, I would get wet either way. The waterproofs would eventually become too saturated, and the water would just seep through. Or, due to my jacket not being that breathable, I would sweat underneath and get damp. Either way, I felt if I had them on, it wouldn't be as bad. But only a few minutes later, the light rain decided to stop. So, it was off again with the waterproofs!

After following the B9176 around the western side of Cnoc Corr Guinie, the road led into a much-needed long descent, joining up near to the A9. Then, I headed along the B817, passing through Evanton and before reaching Dingwall. It was at this point, the rain returned with a vengeance, and it began to hammer it down.

This time there was no messing about, the waterproofs were on in seconds, and I was soaked. Knowing that I was supposed to be wild camping tonight filled me with dread. The thought of carrying out wet and dry drills, changing into dry clothes during the night and putting wet gear back on in the morning did not spark any enthusiasm in me whatsoever!

At Dingwall, the route headed left along a cycle path following alongside the A835. After crossing the River Conon, it was then a combination of back roads and cycle path running parallel with the A835 and A9, leading down to Kessock Bridge. I did chuckle to myself when passing a large road sign displaying a warning for severe weather for the weekend. Fortunately, the closer I got to Inverness, much of the rain had dissipated, and it remained dry for the remainder of the afternoon and evening.

Once over the other side, I made my way to the River Ness, heading through Inverness city centre, only managing to take the wrong direction twice. Nevertheless, I navigated my way through pretty quickly. Following the book, the route then led out towards Culloden. Nearby to here is Culloden Battlefield, which I didn't get to see, unfortunately. After arriving at Balloch, I turned right onto Culloden Road, into a long climb. Eventually, it got to the point where I had completely exhausted all of my energy levels. Apart from the bags of Haribo and café stop back in Ardgay; the only meal of the day had been the large breakfast at The Crask Inn. So, I was pretty much running on empty at this point.

After a while, I began to approach a wooded area where I noticed a small

My first night wild camping

turning area and grassy roundabout, seemingly used by buses judging by the bus stop. Completely exhausted, I threw myself onto the grassy roundabout, spread-eagled, and laid there staring up at the sky. A short time later, I looked around and discovered close by a track leading into the woodland. After deciding I was done entirely for the day, I went into the woods for closer investigation and thought it seemed like an excellent place to camp for the night. It was around the location that I had planned on getting to, so I was happy with the progress I had made for the day. I quickly set up camp, made dinner, boiled rice and tuna while scoffing a few other snacks and got my head down for the night.

Day 04
Inverness to Aviemore - 34.60 mi (55.68 km)

After I'd set up camp, little did I know that I'd be in for a poor night's sleep. Throughout the night, I had to make emergency alterations to my basha, as I was getting soaked. After just a few hours of broken sleep, I eventually woke to the patter of rain once again. By this point, it was turning into a real miserable experience; here I was camped out in woods on the outskirts of Inverness, still damp from the day before with hardly any sleep. To make matters worse, it must have been about 4:30 in the morning.

While still snuggled up in my cocoon-like sleeping bag, I checked the weather for the day. It was not looking good; more torrential rain! I decided I didn't want to face another night in the wild after another day of getting soaked. So, I searched for accommodation, and to my absolute delight, I managed to book myself one of the last of two beds available at Aviemore Hostel. Someone was certainly looking out for me, I thought to myself.

When wrapped up in a warm, snug, sleeping bag, it takes a tremendous amount of will power to get out in the rain and pack up all your gear. But after laying there for another three hours, I eventually decided to get round around 8:00 am. That said, I wasn't too hard on myself as it was only going to be a short distance compared to other days, and check-in wasn't until 3:00 pm.

No sooner as I had stepped out from the woods, the rain had started its onslaught again. I pulled over to put my damp waterproofs on and continued onwards, head down, thinking to myself I couldn't have chosen a better week to do this!

The route passed next by Clava Cairns. And after reading up on it beforehand, I wanted to stop and have a proper look. But since the heavens had opened and it was raining heavily, I peered from my seat at the large, Bronze age, circular tombs and slowly cycled past. Shortly after, I made a right turn into an incline. Despite the rain, a beautiful view greeted me from a distance, with the impressive Culloden Viaduct stretching 1800 feet across the landscape. The view alone was enough to take my mind off the climb. Once I'd reached the top, I then joined up with the Highland Main Line, running between Inverness and Aviemore, before heading along to arrive at the B9154.

After an initial climb out of Craggie and with the rain easing off, it felt like a leisurely ride as I approached Moy, bypassing Loch Moy on my left. The route then followed close to the A9 for another 4 miles passing through Tomatin, where to my disappointment, I was unable to stock up on sweets at the village shop due to it being closed. I then rejoined the A9 and continued alongside it, although out of sight to the A9, over to Carrbridge. I remarked this section was a real joy to cycle on with the far-off reaching hills either side of me, panoramic views in the distance, and stunning woodland surroundings making for a remarkable cycle.

Arriving at Carrbridge, the rain had once again returned. I did consider, as my eyes darted at the numerous cafes, to stop. But I decided against it and sped straight through until I reached the A95. I then turned left as I made my way over to the small village, Boat of Garten. This time I did spot a café. And since I still had time to kill and I was so close to Aviemore, I decided to stop for lunch and give myself the chance to get out of the pouring rain.

The jacket potato, coffee, and cake I opted for indeed went down well. But it wasn't long until I pressed on, along the final 5.6-mile stretch into Aviemore, consisting of winding paths along the NCN Route 7, with plenty of natural surroundings including heather-covered moorland and dense forest. Along the journey, I even got a glimpse of the passing steam train, bellowing its way along the Strathspey Railway to Broomhill.

I got to Aviemore with an hour still to kill before check-in. I sat on the bench in the main car park, pleased with my progress to date. I managed to sort out some admin, dispose of my rubbish, then pressed on to the hostel. As soon as I got there, I placed my bike in the bike store for safekeeping. Then, off I went to my room to be greeted by a wonderfully comfy bed. It was then a quick change out of my wet gear which all went into the drying room. I have to say that as far as hostels go, I was seriously impressed with Aviemore Hostel. I highly recommend staying there, as the facilities are superb!

One of the great things about staying in hostels is that you get to meet a diverse range of people. Throughout the afternoon and evening, I got chatting with an Erika from Australia, Linus from Munich, who was also sharing a room with me, and Cameron. We all went for a drink at a local pub, and I had a good time chatting with you all. It was a pleasure meeting you guys!

Day 05
Aviemore to Pitlochry - 59.47 mi (95.70 km)

After an all-you-can-eat breakfast at the hostel (I certainly tried to eat as much as I could), I followed the same routine - loading up my bike ready for the day ahead as well as oiling the chain. I managed to catch Erika, Linus, and Cameron in the morning, before departing and saying goodbye. Setting off, I felt fantastic - I was well-rested, well-fed, and there were even glimpses of the sun shining in the sky.

Leaving Rothiemurchus

Leaving Aviemore, my route led down to the roundabout. Then a left turn along to Iverdruie, then onto the B970. Cycling along this road was a stunningly beautiful route to pass along, with woodland on either side of the road, occasionally bypassing the odd house. What a fantastic place to live, I thought to myself.

I had travelled this road by car, some years prior. We took a trip to Inshriach Nursery to check out the tearooms. This place was indeed a hidden gem in the heart of the Rothiemurchus. Although famous for their cakes (which were astoundingly delicious), the best part was the conservatory that looked out towards several bird feeders that hung between the trees. I remember the enjoyable experience of having never seen so many birds feeding, with hundreds of different species waiting to get stuck into the bird feeders. Even red squirrels got in on the action; they would scurry down the trees, load up on nuts, and scamper back off, before repeating the process. I could have stayed for hours watching this hive of activity. But after researching the place before my trip, I sadly discovered that the nursery had since closed.

The route continued to Kingussie, along the A86 to Newtonmore, which is where the trail joins up with the A9. The plan from here was to follow the A9 alongside the left-hand side of the Cairngorms. Following this route, I would eventually reach Pitlochry. If you've not carried out any research or were wondering which course to take, I would say to avoid this way if possible. Even more so if you're on a road bike, as the quality of the A9 cycle path was horrendous, with broken tarmac in a lot of places. It was at this point; I was grateful for having a mountain bike, as it genuinely came into its own.

It wasn't long until joining the A9 cycle path that I had an experience that I would rather not relive. I arrived at a layby where construction workers were carrying out resurfacing to the cycle path. One of them informed me I couldn't proceed along the cycle path and would have to go along the A9. It took me a few seconds to register. I looked at the traffic, trucks and cars were hurtling past, in both directions. I thought did I just hear him correctly.

Nevertheless, I waited to cross to the opposite side. This process seemed to take a while due to the sheer amount of traffic on the road. But after a while, I eventually made it across and made it well out of the way of traffic. However, during the crossing, my water bottle decided to jump out of the front bottle cage. I turned to see it rolling in the road close to the side a few metres back. But, by this point, it was too late. A massive lorry was quickly approaching. So, I decided it was best not to go back for it and sacrifice the bottle.

I let the lorry pass and continued on the stony verge at the side, keeping away from the road. This surface turned out to be too bumpy and impossible to cycle on. So, I quickly decided to re-enter the road and cycled a few hundred metres down the A9. After I had passed the construction workers over to the far side, I thought to myself - sod this. I crossed back over to continue along the cycle path, well away from the main road. The best thing about taking this route was the descent which started roughly after the large sign displaying 'Slochd Summit 1315 ft (401 m) above sea level'. To my delight, it was downhill for a very long way afterwards.

During my planning phase, a friend recommended that I visit The House of Bruar. After carrying out research, I discovered that I definitely should! My route happened to pass right past the entrance, so I ensured to factor in a stop. The House of Bruar is an upscale department store with the most magnificent food hall I have ever seen. There's a vast range of drinks, cheeses, cured meats, fish, the list is endless.

I arrived at the entrance, locked my bike up, and immediately proceeded to the fish and chip shop as I had been craving fish and chips since setting off. It was certainly worth it, and it was the perfect treat for my efforts. Next, it was straight across the road to explore the aisles and aisles of food delights. As soon as I walked through the door, the biggest grin beamed from my face; my eyes couldn't keep still - continually darting from one thing to another. I could have spent an absolute fortune in here if I wanted to. Luckily, I was short on space. So, in the end, I only came away with a pack of biscuits, some Scottish tea, a pork pie, and a scotch egg from the deli. Although, I must admit that the temptation was there to empty my panniers and fill it full of delights!

After setting off, a huge moment of inconvenience happened, something that took me by total surprise. As I went to pedal, the chain decided to come away. I looked down and could feel the thought of dread slowly building. Here I was, still 10 miles from Pitlochry and my chain decides to come away. Just my luck, I thought.

I then calmly made my may back to the cycle park and replaced the broken link (that had become completely bent backwards) with a split link. Soon enough, I was back on my way. But just as I thought I was back on track, the rain conveniently decided to return. After a short while, this turned into a torrential downpour. So, by the time I reached Pitlochry Hostel, I was thoroughly drenched.

Arriving at Pitlochry

After a warm welcome at check-in, I placed my bike in storage, my wet kit went in the drying room, and I headed to the local Co-Op to stock up on supplies. I would have liked to explore more of Pitlochry as it was set in a beautiful location, surrounded by Perthshire's Highlands. Plus, as the hostel was perched high up above the town, the dining room provided a fantastic panoramic view while I was gorging on food, planning my route for the next day.

Day 06
Pitlochry to The Trossachs - 67.41 mi (108.48 km)

As the hostel provided breakfast, I thought it would be rude to not take them up on the offer once again, especially as you could practically eat as much as you like. It was the same as in Aviemore. Various cereals, a selection of ham, bread rolls, Danish pastries, fruit, and copious amounts of coffee. I made sure to eat as much as I could to get my money's worth. After I enjoyed such a hearty breakfast, I saddled up and headed off once again.

On setting off, I made my way down to the main road that led through Pitlochry and crossed over the Iron suspension bridge. My route followed along the NCN route 7, running alongside the River Tummel. To my right, Dunfallandy Hill rose high into the sky, complete with its beautiful wooded hillsides. But there was no way of getting over this, other than heading around the south-eastern side of the hill to the west of Logierait. From here, the route headed west alongside the River Tay to Kenmore.

My plan was for Kenmore to be a well-earned rest stop, as the village located at the northern end of the 14-mile loch looked beautifully idyllic. There was even the perfect bench situated at the shoreline providing a picturesque view out over the visible area of the loch, with Ben Lawers standing high in the distance. However, no sooner as I arrived at the bench, I breathed a huge sigh of disappointment - praying if there would ever be any let-up. Rolling down off the side of the mountain was a large formation of rain clouds, and you could see the heavy rain heading straight towards me. So much for relaxing by the loch, I thought. To keep myself dry, I had my waterproofs on in seconds, and I decided it was best not to hang around.

The road continued along the southern edge of the loch. Fortunately, I didn't get too wet in the end. Upon reaching the halfway point, I decided to have a short break overlooking the loch and even took pleasure in devouring a couple of chocolate bars and a can of fizzy pop to keep my fuelled up for the ride ahead. To my pleasant surprise, the sun even decided to make an appearance, so I certainly made the most of this for a few short minutes.

It was a relief to make the western edge of the loch and pass south of the village of Killin. Fourteen miles doesn't sound like much on a bike, but the loch seemed never-ending. Before my turn off, I noticed a bench next to the Killin's War Memorial, with the River Dochart running close by. It was the memorial that caught my eye the most, as it was a beautifully carved stone statue of a Scottish soldier, stood on a plinth with the inscription of all the names of those who lost their lives in both World Wars. After taking the time to pay my respects, I took a seat and ate the goodies I had purchased the day before at The House of Bruar, ever conscious of the gloomy overcast clouds that could pour down with rain at any second.

Killin memorial lunch stop

As always, I didn't stop too long. I still had a fair distance to cover, intending to get as close to Aberfoyle as possible. From the bench, I headed a few metres back and up a gravel track, doubling up with the Rob Roy Way, a hiking trail. At the tip of Lochan Lairig Cheile, the route merged into another trail, The Glen Ogle Trail, and it was at this point, I was in for a treat. The path followed an old railway line from Lochearnhead. Luckily for me going in the opposite direction, it was downhill all the way. Being quite high up, I sped down from the mountainside, captured by the breath-taking scenery over to my left comprising of a panoramic view of Loch Earn and Ben Our, a famous Munro.

After the exhilarating descent, it was round to Strathyre, keeping to the cycle trail, weaving through areas of woodland and open land, exposing Loch Voil River as it snaked nearby. It was not long after that my bike decided to start making a clicking sound with each turn of the crank. I pulled up at a bench to perform a quick maintenance check. To my horror, a pin had come away from the link and was just about holding on. After a few curse words, I managed to fix it quickly, which put my mind at rest. I also took the opportunity to search for any bike shops on route. I thought it might be a good idea to buy a new chain before any more links decided to give out.

Climbing back into the saddle, I pressed on to make my way around Loch Lubnaig before passing through Forest Holidays Strathyre, a popular holiday park. The trail ran right through the middle of the park and is where I met Jacob. He stopped me and enquired as to where I was heading. I told him about my trip, and he very kindly helped me fix the issue with my chain. It turned out that he was the bicycle mechanic at the park, and I couldn't believe my luck! Struan, a friend of Jacob, also appeared and he very kindly rode with me to Callander and even offered to sort me out a room in the local hostel.

With nightfall fast approaching, I needed to get as close to Aberfoyle as I could. Otherwise, I'd have to make up the extra distance in the morning. So as kind as the offer was, I kindly declined a room in the hostel, deciding I would ride until last light if need be. From Callander, the route led west past the western edge of Loch Venachar. By this point, I was now very low on energy. And since I knew there was a steepish climb approaching, I thought I would get it over and done with as opposed to attempting it in the morning.

After heading along Forest Drive, I reached a gravel road running through an area of the Trossachs. I came to a large parking area, with a toilet block. I decided this would be the perfect place to camp, so I immediately set about finding a decent patch of woodland to set up my tarp. After a few minutes of running about the area searching, I had managed to find a relatively flat piece of land with two trees the perfect distance apart for properly setting up my tarp. The spot also provided enough cover from the rain. And so, once my basha was erected, I sat back to relax, pleased with my efforts for the day.

While cooking tea, the standard boiled rice and tuna, I had a friend join me. But not as you would expect, it was a little robin that came and greeted me, hopping from branch to branch, occasionally landing on the front wheel right in front of me. As I was eating a bag of fruit and nut mix, I decided it was only fair to share. He stayed with me for some time and continued hopping about the place, chirping away until the darkness came.

An evening meal, wild camping in The Trossachs

Day 07
The Trossachs to New Lanark - 84.07 mi (135.29 km)

The evening before, I thought I had made it over the highest point. But as it turned out, I hadn't, much to my disappointment. To make matters worse, I still had quite a way to venture before reaching Aberfoyle. Because of this, I decided to skip breakfast, mostly because I didn't fancy another tuna and rice dish. So, I decided to press on early in the morning and pick something up in Aberfoyle. But given that making it up and over the final hill proved tough, I would live to regret this decision, with my energy levels all-but depleted. Luckily for me, once I had reached the peak of the climb, it was a fast descent into the village.

By the time I reached the main road, I had arrived at the door of the local Co-Op where I had stopped to pick up supplies—mainly water along with breakfast consisting of three pastries. In hindsight, I really should have bought more food on this particular occasion.

Little did I know, the route out of Aberfoyle and the proceeding section to Lanark would go on to become one of the hardest rides and most significant tests of mental resilience that I've ever had to put myself through.

From the moment I left Aberfoyle, the route headed southwest to Balloch, via Drymen. Only a few miles out from Aberfoyle, my chain started making noises again, so I pulled over to investigate. My heart sunk as I made the unwanted discovery of another loose chain link. I swiftly replaced it with another spare link, managing to bend the pin on the chain tool at the same time. Given that this issue had happened more than once, I was starting to run low on spare links. Thankfully, I had no further problems with my chain for the rest of the journey as a whole. But, I still couldn't help that had any more broken, I could have been in deep trouble.

It was just before reaching Balloch that another potential disaster began. With a turn of the crank, a sharp shooting pain in the muscle just above my left knee took hold. Eager to press on, I occasionally rubbed it. But it was no use, as with each turn, the pain only worsened.

After the previous calamity of bending the tip of my chain tool, I stopped off at Magic Cycles. It was here I thought it would be wise to buy a new chain and chain tool just in case, along with a water bottle to replace the one that I lost on the A9. And of course, coffee to provide some much-needed fuel. I attempted a quick shake off and a few stretches, but it didn't do much. Nevertheless, I still had a long way to go, and I was determined to carry on despite the fact the pain seemed to be getting worse as I went on!

After setting off again, I was following a canal path down to and through Glasgow, with nothing too exciting happening. I just got my head down and tried to make up the distance, trying not to apply too much pressure with my left leg. At least the route was flat since it followed alongside the River Clyde. I managed to make it through Uddingston and Hamilton, but given my current speed and the pain I was in, I would struggle to make the check-in at the hostel.

I arrived at Chatelherault rail station and wondered if I could get the train to Lanark. However, when looking at the destination of the next station and saw that it was only going approximately 2 miles down the line to Larkhall, I decided against it. Besides, I didn't want to cheat; no matter small the distance was. So, I pressed on in agony. But just as I thought things couldn't get any worse, my other knee started hurting!

I don't quite know how, but I somehow eventually reached New Lanark, making check-in. It had been the longest ride of my life at 84 miles. For the most part, I was pedalling the whole way, mainly using my right leg while only applying slight pressure with the left. However, upon reaching New Lanark, all of the agony and mental anguish had been completely obliterated, I was sky-high on endorphins. Nevertheless, I was exhausted, having completed such a mammoth journey eating just three pastries, a bag of Haribo and a coffee along the way.

I couldn't believe that in this beautiful world heritage site, there was a hostel that cost less than £40 for the night. The best part was I had a large room with a double bed and walk-in shower all to myself, a night of heaven. The room might have been on the top floor and the furthest away from the entrance. But it didn't matter; I was grateful to have a warm, comfortable place to stay.

As the heritage site is at the bottom of a deep valley, during check-in, I was horrified to discover that the nearest supermarket was back up the steep hill I had come down, a 20-minute walk away. I did phone a taxi company to get a lift, but the guy's accent on the other end was indecipherable. I just about managed to hear him say it would be about 20 minutes, so in the end, I decided that I would walk after all.

In need of supplies, I dropped my kit off to the room before starting the walk back up the hill. I bought an obscene amount of food from Morrisons, picking up all manner of things that looked appetising, including deep heat. I even went and picked up a battered sausage and chips from the nearby chippy. Needless to say, I ate like a king that night, and nothing went to waste!

Day 08
New Lanark to Gretna - 68.08 mi (109.56 km)

Upon waking, my mind immediately wondered if my night's rest and excellent sleep would have been enough to semi-heal the pain experienced in both my knees. From the comfort of my bed, I had a good look at the route I would be following for the day. With a 68-mile journey ahead of me, it would be a case of following the NCN Route 74, linking Glasgow to the border. The route pretty much ran alongside the A74(M), all the way down to the border. A nice straight forward ride, I thought. A bonus is that I would have nearly completed Scotland since it was so close to the border.

I didn't want to make the same mistake after leaving the Trossachs National Park, the previous day. So, I ensured that I had double helpings of porridge at breakfast. Naturally, I put off leaving the hostel as long as possible, making the most of having a lie-in and leaving bang on at the checkout time.

Once everything was attached, there was no other route out of New Lanark than to ascend the only, steep, road that led out of the steep valley. There was no way I was cycling up that fully laden, I thought to myself. Instead, I opted to push the bike to the top.

Reaching the main road which ran through Lanark, it was a short descent down to and over the River Clyde, through Kirkfieldbank. Once over the bridge and after a swift left turn, I was back onto the familiar quiet undulating country lanes, making my way south to a junction with the M74.

At reaching the M74, passing underneath, I continued my way along the B7078. Although there was a dedicated cycle lane marked by a white line, kind of like a hard shoulder, it was an incredibly fast road with the occasional car or lorry hurtling past. I firmly stayed as close to the verge as possible. I was making slow progress, and despite a large breakfast, my legs were incredibly fatigued.

Thankfully, after just over a mile, I got off of the main road since there was a dedicated cycle path running parallel. I could finally relax and enjoy the experience, taking in the views of the surrounding vast open moorland, all without the need to worry about traffic racing past.

It was about halfway along this path when the dreaded pain in both knees returned to punish me. I had a bit of a search the night before to try and get some answers, and I put it down to overuse after the never-ending turns of the crank. In some instances, it became unbearable, but my left was still worse than my right, so again I found myself pedalling using one leg for the most part - ever grateful for the downhill sections that I could slowly coast along. Now and again, I'd take a short break and apply copious amounts of deep heat to the area, hoping it would provide some respite. In fairness, it did numb the pain slightly, but not for very long.

Arriving at Abington provided a big motivational boost. I got off of the B7078 and was roughly a quarter of the way closer to my destination. My next target was to get past a place called Elvanfoot, located on the opposite side of the River Clyde.

After checking the profile of the terrain for my route, I knew that a few miles past Elvanfoot, it would be downhill to Westlands Country Park, my destination. Although I would still have to pedal, it certainly made the remainder of the 40 or so miles glorious. It felt a breeze to coast most of the route, despite adding a couple of unnecessary miles after taking a wrong turn at the village of Beattock, where I had got mixed up with another cycle route.

After passing through Lockerbie, it was onwards through to Ecclefechan and Kirtlebridge where I made a left turn onto the quiet country lanes, making my way towards the campsite. The weather had even come out for the finale of the leg, and the evening was glorious. It was the first bit of proper sunshine since setting off.

On reaching Westlands Country Park, my campsite, I was greeted by the friendliest and most welcoming of staff. After pitching, I carried out the usual tasks of sorting out admin, getting clean, and preparing dinner. I even managed to bask in the sun on the smooth lawn where I had set up camp. A special mention goes to Aaron, who went out of

Camping at Westlands Country Park

his way to make me feel extremely welcome, letting me watch tv and chatting until I turned in for the night.

Day 09
Gretna to King's Meaburn - 54.86 mi (88.28 km)

I awoke around 5:00 am to the patter of rain on my tarp, yet again. This time it was terrible, I cursed the miserable weather. I had already endured so much rain, so all I wanted was just a few days of normal, dry weather. Was it was too much to ask to have a few dry days? Nevertheless, I needed to press on, but I didn't want to ride on an empty stomach. So I boiled some rice for breakfast - huddled and pressed up against my bike as I attempted to keep dry.

Crossing the border

That said, by now I had become so unfazed by the bad weather, I just accepted it. So, I gathered my strength and managed to pull myself from the vice-like grip of my sleeping bag and preceded with a sense of urgency in packing everything away, as the rain had become a lot harsher.

Today I planned to reach the small village of Orton, 8 miles from Appleby-in-Westmoreland, or at least get as close to it as possible. I noted that the elevation was the complete opposite of yesterday, it was going to be an ascent pretty much the entire journey to Penrith. With everything secured, I set off out of the campsite and headed on to Gretna and towards the border.

After getting a mile down the road from Leaving Westlands Country Park, I discovered I had left my bungee cords back at the pitch! Without as much as a grumble, I stoically did an about-turn and cycled back to recover them. I couldn't have abandoned them as I had no accommodation booked for the night and would be wild camping. They were essential for tying the ends of my tarp.

With the bungees recovered and secured, off I went again. With the rain fiercely lashing down, I made my way into the south of Gretna, making the decision to stop at a convenience store to pick up some supplies, consisting of cakes and a much-needed coffee. The weather was so miserable I just wanted to plod on, so didn't I hang about.

I knew it was nearby, but not long after Gretna, I was pleasantly surprised to arrive at the English/Scottish border. Of course, I had to get the customary photo of my bike propped up against the sign. It was also a moment of reflection; I had just ridden the entire length of Scotland. I was now crossing into England and about to take on the homeward stretch.

The route I was following from the book took a very long detour up through Longtown. There was no way I was interested in adding unnecessary mileage onto my journey, so I decided to cut along the side road running parallel to the M6, passing over the Channel of River Esk, a much quicker way to reach Carlisle.

Eventually, I arrived at a level crossing, along with two cars. By this point, the rain hadn't in the slightest died down. What followed was the longest wait I have ever experienced at a level crossing. But my only option was to balance on my bike and hold onto a post, waiting patiently.

I kept peering left and right, keeping my eyes peeled for any sign of trains. After a few minutes, a train did come hurting down the track. I thought great that was it, expecting the barriers to lift soon, yet nothing. I sat here for what seemed like an eternity waiting for another train to appear. It was during this period, completely soaked to the bone, the rain continued to pour the hardest it had been. I had no warm accommodation booked for the evening, and I sat there wondering what on earth I was doing with my life.

As soon as the barrier lifted, I let the cars go ahead then went on my way, pushing the negative thoughts out of my mind. After rounding a corner, I passed a female cyclist going in the opposite direction, who shouted words to the effect of "We must be mad!", bringing a smile to my face. I suddenly perked up at this point, realising at least I wasn't the only one out here.

Before I knew it, I was in front of Carlisle Castle and took respite underneath the sheltered steps of the footbridge, crossing the road. Here, I reminisced on my previous brief encounter with Carlisle, when I attempted to walk Hadrian's wall path some years prior, only making it halfway across due to me picking up an injury.

This time in Carlisle was also set to be a brief visit, as I didn't want to waste too much time. My route took me south, heading along the River Caldew and over to Dalston. Then, I'd head south-east through the quiet country lanes to Penrith. Thankfully, the rain had died off, but I prepared myself for its return at any moment.

Around late afternoon, I found myself wandering aimlessly around the centre of Penrith. Food was on my mind while I was here after the awful weather I'd endured so far today. Luckily, I came across the local Greggs store where I had my mind set on buying the lot! Well, not quite everything, but I indeed came away with a lot - meat pies, pastry slices, cakes, and a coffee. I sat down to enjoy my mini feast on a bench just outside the bakery, sharing with a couple of pigeons, much to the amusement of a nearby child.

With the evening fast approaching and another night of wild camping ahead of me, I was conscious of the time as I still had quite a distance to cover. So, I made my way down through the villages of

Great Strickland, then over to Morland and soon found myself wandering through King's Meaburn.

By this point, it was lashing down again, with the darkness creeping in and my energy all but zapped. As I passed by the White Horse Inn, that's where I spotted it, a stone bus shelter. I went in for a closer inspection, inside was a bench full of books, still enough room to sit down. That's it I thought, I'm not moving. I decided it would be the perfect place to get my head down for the night—a readymade shelter.

Not long after, a friendly couple visiting the pub pulled up in the car park in front of me and came over and chatted for a few minutes. They kindly invited me in for a drink, but regrettably, I declined as I was worried about leaving my bike alone. As soon as it was dark, I blew up my roll mat, hung my soaking wet clothing up and crawled into my sleeping bag still damp from the day and fell fast asleep.

My accommodation for the night

No sooner as I had drifted off, a lady woke me while dropping off the morning papers for the villagers on the bench behind me. I immediately sprang up and apologised. Apparently, it was quite a common sight for her to find cyclists sleeping in bus shelters.

Day 10
King's Meaburn to Forest of Bowland - 60.21 mi (96.89 km)

Today's cycle would be to the Forest of Bowland. Again, I had no accommodation booked, but I knew that I wanted to reach somewhere with some trees, preferably Slaidburn. Due to the lady dropping the papers off, it crossed my mind the villagers would soon be over collecting them. I thought I would make a swift exit before anyone arrived, so I decided to skip breakfast on this occasion. I saw there was a café in Orton, so I'd stop there instead.

I packed everything away and started to attach my bags, shortly after discovering that my front wheel was completely flat. How could this have happened? I thought. The bike hadn't moved all night, and it was perfectly fine before I fell asleep. I pumped it up, thinking it would be fine and headed down the lane. No sooner as I got a few hundred metres down the road, the wheel was flat again. Why I thought it would be fine, I don't know.

What should have been a quick change of the inner tube turned into over an hour wasted, fussing about. First, I decided that it would be best to go back to where I was initially because at least I could sit down on the bench. I pumped air into the flat wheel and headed back along the lane to the shelter, only for the wheel to go flat again rather quickly. So I propped my bike up against the gate of a nearby field before changing the tube. Luckily, the weather had decided to be kind.

Once I successfully changed the tube, it occurred to me that the back might have lost some air, during my journey so far. So, I thought it might be a good idea to pump it up a little. After topping it up, I went to undo the hose connector, and the uppermost part of the valve core came away from the main body, with all the air gushing out! I couldn't believe it, as this happened at least twice. Screwing the core back into the body, I then pumped the tyre up and tried to take the pump hose off without it coming away again. In the end, I employed the help of pliers to tighten the valve and repeated the process, this time successfully.

I did eventually manage to get on my way, making it to Orton, stopping in Orton Scar Café - a popular stop on the Coast to Coast walk, where enjoyed a slap-up fry up. Leaving Orton, I headed west towards the M6. Along the way, I passed under the southbound carriage and found myself in-between the centre, much like a no man's land between the north and southbound carriages. I preceded up a service road about half a mile before realising I was going the wrong way. I should have crossed under both carriages. I put these errors down to being tired.

Once I was heading in the correct direction, I made my way through the hamlets of Greenholme, down through Roundthwaite. Following quiet roads alongside the M6, I eventually reached the other side of the motorway, where the road ran high above, providing a fantastic vantage point down through the valley. From the village of Beck Foot, I continued west and skirted around the eastern outskirts of Kendal, to Natland.

From Natland, I reached the pretty village of Beetham, which is where I stumbled across a delightful little shop with a Tea Room. Sadly, the Tea Room had just closed, so I was left with what little the shop offered, only stocking up on the usual sugar-laden treats of cakes, sweets, and cans of pop, thinking it would be enough. Opposite the shop was a churchyard. Since the sun had come out, I made the most of it and parked up at the bench in the church's grounds. Sprawled across the bench exhausted, I grabbed a precious few minutes of relaxation.

Leaving Beetham, I encountered a very steep hill climb, which I didn't have the energy to take on. So, I found myself pushing my bike up the hill for the most part. A short distance after Slackhead, I found myself yet again heading in the wrong direction, adding an unnecessary mile on top of what I already had to cover. After the error, I made my way over to and through Borwick, Gressingham, and Hornby. Passing through Hornby, I remarked at what a beautiful place it was. The stone buildings looked beautiful, indeed.

I continued to pass through Wray and Mill Houses until I arrived at a crossroad and instantly spotted another stone sheltered bus stop. I thought of having another night of luxury and making the shelter my home. But, in the end, I decided against it as Slaidburn was still another 13 miles away. Any extra distance I could make up now would mean covering fewer miles the following morning.

Wild Camping in the Forest of Bowland

A little further up the road from the shelter, I came across a dense patch of woodland. Here, I spent some time looking at the map and saw that this was probably the best I was going to get for the night, and it would provide a bit of protection from the elements. By this point, I was again devoid of energy. So, I entered the woodland and quickly set about making a shelter, conscious of keeping a low profile.

Day 11
Forest of Bowland to Manchester - 65.75 mi (105.81 km)

As was always the case when wild camping, I had yet another night of tossing and turning. Nevertheless, it was time to make a move. There was no point in putting it off, so I was straight up and had my gear packed within minutes. Checking the map, I saw there was a Tearoom in Slaidburn, so I decided I would skip breakfast again. However, it was still 13 miles away, which was a considerable distance on my heavily laden machine.

Upon stumbling out of the trees onto the road, I instantly felt mentally and physically drained, with not even the slightest bit of energy inside me whatsoever. I ate the last few sweets I picked up the day before and drank a can of fizzy pop in one gulp, hoping it would provide the energy I needed to get to Riverbank Tearooms.

I set off pedalling at a slow pace before taking on a 6-mile ascent I needed to conquer before the descent into Slaidburn. Those 6 miles were quite possibly the hardest I've ever had to endure, and I have done a lot of physically demanding things! As soon as the incline increased slightly, I climbed out of the saddle and opted to walk - pushing my lumbering beast of a bike, head draped over the bars, taking it one step at a time while having the occasional rest. It is times like this when you have to dig deep, as it is incredibly tempting to give up.

Fortunately, I was in the middle of nowhere, so I had no choice but to press on. I think if there had been a nearby rail station I may have got on a train. But then again, maybe not. Regardless, I was adamant at packing it in once I reached Manchester, getting a train back to Devon the next morning.

Once I struggled over the highest point, I shot down the steep descent in no time at all. But it just led straight into another climb, causing me to get off and push yet again. In the end, the 13 miles to

Slaidburn took me 2 hours. To top it off, just as I got there, it started raining.

To my initial horror, the Tearoom's Wi-Fi was down, so card payments were off. Thankfully, I had cash on me for emergencies, and this was an emergency as I needed food! A massive fry up followed by coffee and cake went down nicely, as I chatted to a guy local to the area, telling me about the epic adventures he had been on in the past.

As I planned my route, I didn't fancy heading up and over Easington Fell to reach Waddington – a small village just north of Clitheroe, where I noted there was a train station. Instead, I decided to stick to the NCN, taking a slight detour passing near to Bolton by Bowland and Grindleton and on through the large village of Whalley.

By the time I set off, I felt rejuvenated entirely, much like having a new lease of life. The fry up had saved me, and I was steaming on my way through to Whalley. It just goes to show how important it is to pack on the calories.

My journey through Whalley eventually crossed over the River Calder and turned left onto Whalley Old Road. Every hill I encountered seemed to be the biggest one. Although this probably wasn't the case, I was in for another massive climb, this time 3 miles, bringing me close to Dean Clough Reservoir. Thankfully, the climb was a breeze, and I was fully charged and didn't stop once to get off and push.

Leeds & Liverpool Canal mural

I then made my way down to the Leeds and Liverpool Canal following it into Accrington. I completely lost the NCN trail signs and spent some time near the train station trying to work out how to get back on the correct path. It turns out I was actually on the path, and I needed to head over the railway line past Tesco, continuing down through the Woodnook Vale Nature reserve, following along an old railway line which has since become a path.

I made my way south, skirting around the eastern side of Haslingden, through into Holcombe Brook before arriving at the north-western corner of Bury town centre, in front of the Peel Memorial. The NCN route signs had once again disappeared, so I had no idea which way to go. So, at this point, I took a seat on a bench and sought directions.

After going in the wrong direction a few hundred metres, through the town, I doubled back, deciding to head south and managed to get back on track. My destination of Salford's Premier Inn now only seemed like it was only around the corner. I was full of energy; the endorphins had undoubtedly kicked in—what an unbelievable change from setting off this morning.

It wasn't long until I passed through the University of Salford and made my way along the final bit of the A6, finally arriving at my hotel for the evening. Of all the places I had stayed, I felt the most welcome at this Premier Inn, as the staff were incredibly accommodating. I chose a night of luxury here as they allow you to take bikes into their rooms. Plus, as it was a Sunday, the room was a lot cheaper.

In the end, I opted to put my bike in the storeroom rather than take it to my room. By this point, my clothes were stinking, and I had been switching between socks since the start. So, I decided it was about time that I did some laundry in the bathroom sink. After a half-assed job, I laid everything out to dry and made my way down to the restaurant and ate like a king - gobbling down a three-course meal. But given the number of calories I'd burnt; it didn't even touch the sides. Regardless, the food was sublime, and I had a night of luxury ahead of me in a comfy double bed.

Day 12
Manchester to Bridgnorth - 88.88 mi (143.03 km)

As soon as I woke, I scurried down for breakfast, devouring as much food as I could. Today was going to be a massive ride, so I ate an enormous fry-up, had a few bowls of cereal, a load of Danishes, along with multiple cups of coffee to wash it all down.

I collected my bike from the storeroom, but rather than get the foyer covered in mud and oil; I decided it would be best to take it outside to fit all the panniers and oil my chain properly. Considering the state of it, it was surprisingly holding up very well.

Today, the Sustrans cycle book I was following went entirely out the window. I certainly didn't want to be taking the scenic route by adding a lot of mileage on my already massive ride. I checked the night before and thankfully, Google Maps loaded me a route that followed along the canal path down to Broadheath.

Setting off from the hotel, I made my way along the Bridgewater Canal Towpath. Naturally, I had set off during rush hour, and it became a case of dodging people walking along the towpath on their way to work. Thankfully, as I headed further away from Salford, the number of commuters diminished. The canal ran directly behind Old Trafford, literally within

Knitted JOGLE sign

striking distance, so I took an obligatory photograph and pressed on to Broadheath, to the south-west of Manchester city centre.

Just after Broadheath, I joined onto the Trans Pennine Trail, which was just under a 5 km, dead flat, straight line. On arriving at the main road, I had a lovely surprise; someone had knitted a blue sign with JOGLE written in white and attached it to the gate. I couldn't believe it! Did someone know I was coming? I thought as I chuckled to myself.

I headed south and made my way over the M6 for the final time, surprised to arrive at Northwich. This was my first psychological marker, and it felt like I had reached it in no time at all, with ease! Passing through Northwich, the trail followed alongside the beautiful River Weaver, all the way down to Winsford.

From Winsford, the route then headed south down to Nantwich along a single country lane. Again, I seemed to cover the distance in no time. I came in from the north and pulled up to an inviting looking wall, next to the town car park. I was at my third checkpoint and more importantly, the halfway mark. Here, I took a 10-minute rest stop while loading up on sugar. I was feeling excellent, with all my worries about not making it to Bridgnorth all but dissipated. Also, the previous day's thoughts of wanting to pack it in coming over the forest of Bowland repulsed me. I can't believe that I even considered packing it in and getting the train home!

My stop in Nantwich was only fleeting. Leaving south-west of the town, I made my way over to Wrenbury, then south-east passing north of Shavington Park, sticking to the country lanes. It was a case of just getting my head down and turning the pedals. Another thing that caught my attention that I hadn't noticed initially was that my knees no longer hurt. Maybe they had finally got used to the abuse they had been put under, or simply given up!

Market Drayton was the next marker, although I passed far to the north. When I finally arrived at the B5062, as I was blindly following the Google Maps route, it decided to take me through the heart of a farm, which led to a dead end. I quickly doubled back, leaving whoever's property it was, with a car following me back down the drive. Thankfully, it was only a slight detour to the next road, which brought me out to where the farm track was supposed to lead.

A few minutes later, I entered into the north of Telford and quickly found myself leaving. It was all cycle path, forming part of the Silkin Way, following dry canal beds and former railway lines. This led all the way down to Coalport, joining up with the River Severn.

By this point, I was getting ever closer to Bridgnorth, approaching the final 6 miles (10 km) of this epic cycle. I made the mistake of having Google Maps on in front of me still. I couldn't help but keep glancing at the distance left to cover, which was a big mistake! I tried to resist the urge to keep looking, at one point I thought I must have covered at least a km, but no, it had only dropped by not more than a couple of hundred metres. The closer I got to Bridgnorth, the distance remaining seemed like it was getting further away! But at least the track was level, I thought to myself.

At the end of the track, I rounded the corner and arrived at North Gate. As soon as I saw the gate, I knew I had made it to Bridgnorth, the sheer joy on my face was yet again euphoric. I had just completed the longest ride of my life, arriving around 5:30 pm with plenty of time to spare. It took me an elapsed time of 9:11 hours. Plus, I had found it incredibly easy. What a difference it makes when you are loaded up with calories to burn.

I quickly found the B&B and got checked in. As always, my bike went in storage, and I headed to my room to get showered. Then, it was time to head out to pick up supplies at the local supermarket, as well as a large portion of fish and chips.

Day 13
Bridgnorth to Gloucester - 74.46 mi (119.83 km)

At each hotel or place that I stayed at, I always made sure to fill up on a hearty breakfast - my stay at The Croft was no exception. I thoroughly enjoyed my stay here after receiving a warm welcome. So, I would certainly recommend staying at this particular B&B. After a large, delicious breakfast, I went to clear out my room and bring my gear down into the foyer.

Here, another couple of guys greeted me, who were cycling the correct way - Land's End to John O'Groats. It then hit me one of them looked vaguely familiar. Do you know when you think you know who someone is but you're not entirely sure? I had an inkling at the back of my mind who it was, but I didn't say anything as we continued to share details on how our journeys had been so far. And, most importantly, what to expect on the proceeding sections.

Later on, I did have to stop and look him up. I searched on the web; he was who I thought it was! I had been chatting to the childhood legend Timmy Mallet and his mate. I remember the previous evening when picking up supplies; I overheard the lady in the local Tesco saying how Timmy Mallet had been in a little earlier. So, to my disappointment, I missed out on getting a photo with the man himself.

Heading off from the B&B, I made my way down to the bank of the River Severn. Along the way, I passed over the historic bridge that links the east and west of the town. After admiring the scenery, I plotted my route on Google Maps and headed south out of the village along the B4555. It was only a short distance from leaving the town that I encountered the first hill of the morning. And despite being well-rested and fully fuelled, my legs were as heavy as lead, and my speed soon dropped to a slow crawl. With my legs as they were, I did think if this was the sign of things to come. Thankfully, Timmy and his mate did assure me that the route to Gloucester was reasonably flat.

After roughly two miles, I managed to get off the B4555, back onto the quiet country lanes and made my way to the small hamlet of Hampton Loade, by-passing the heritage railway station, which forms part of the Severn Valley Railway heritage line. The trail continued south, practically running parallel with the railway on my right and River Severn to my left. It was on down to the Severn Valley Country Park where it was a steep climb up to the visitor

Mercian way marker

centre. Thankfully, the sun had now come out so I thought this would be an excellent opportunity for a short rest on one of the benches, overlooking the beautiful valley.

Pressing on through country lanes, believing the worst of the hills were over, it wasn't long until I descended into the village of Upper Arley, that sits on the north bank of the River Severn. A footbridge at the base of the hill links the village to the opposite side, where Arley railway station is based. The station, built in 1862, serves as a stop on a section of the heritage line, and it has even been featured in many films and tv shows. I did take a quick look at the station from the bridge and remarked at how immaculate it all looked. I also needed to have a breather, as the incline out of the valley was again extremely steep. In the end, I found myself walking up another hill. As I struggled, a group of older cyclists came whizzing up past, wishing me a good morning with words of encouragement.

As soon as the road levelled out, I was back in the saddle, heading south to Buttonoak, a small village situated in the Wyre Forest. It was then a case of following along the B4194 into Bewdley, a very picturesque riverside town. It was a place that I would have liked to have taken some time to explore with a stroll along the riverside. But as I had a lot of miles to cover, I pressed on.

Passing over the River Severn again, I continued along the B4195, until finding my way back on to the country paths. It then led me through Burlish Top Nature Reserve, passing first through Stourport-on-Severn before I made my way along quiet country lanes to Droitwich Spa. After this, I was able to follow the well-signposted cycle lanes, which enabled me to make it through fairly quickly.

Once through Droitwich Spa, the route took me close to the M5, even coming to within 100 metres at one point. Despite still being a long way from home, I did sense a small feeling of joy that came over me. The M5 runs to Exeter, and I've driven up and down it so many times, I've always considered it as the home straight. It also reminded me of the distance that I had covered since the start of my journey.

As I continued to follow the route alongside the M5, I then made my way down through the eastern side of Worcester. The trail led along cycle paths that cut through housing estates, until leaving through the south of Worcester. The trail then led me over the opposite side of the M5. Crossing the bridge, I stood in the middle and peered down the motorway thinking, although extremely dangerous, how easy it would be to ride down the hard shoulder, all the way to Exeter.

I pressed on along the tranquil county lanes passing back over the opposite of the M5 for the final time, before making my way into the north of Tewksbury, onwards through Forthampton, over to Hartpury, then arriving at Gloucester Docks.

I was ecstatic upon reaching the docks. Although now wasn't the time for a rest, as I still had to get to the south side of Gloucester. Luckily, my sister had kindly let me stay with her for the night, which turned out to be a perfect planned location stop. This would also be my third night in a row sleeping in accommodation. The remaining five miles were fortunately completely flat along the canal side – making for a very leisurely ride indeed.

Day 14
Gloucester to The Mendips - 64.79 mi (104.26 km)

Tonight, I had planned to stop in the Mendips and wild camp, but I didn't have anywhere booked. So, I had a quick search in the morning for any campsites and managed to find Mendip Camp. Perfect I thought, as it was only £8 to pitch for the night and was in the ideal location, situated just above Cheddar.

After saying goodbye to my sister, her partner, and Rupert (their adorable black pug), I headed off leaving about 08:30 am. I quickly popped to Tesco then made my way through Quedgeley, back to the Gloucester Canal and following it south. It was quite a nice change to be able to follow a completely flat route for the first part of the day.

I made my way through Frampton on Severn, taking a small deviation from the canal, then on down to Sheperd's Patch. Here, I

left the canal and continued along quiet roads to Berkeley, onwards down through to Olveston. Nothing much exciting happened, but it was an absolute joy to cycle along, as I remarked at the beauty of the area. As it was approaching lunch, I popped into the local bakery to treat myself to some delicious goodies, including a quiche, cake, and drink. As the weather was beautiful, I went back to the nearby church and relaxed on steps for a short time.

Gloucester Canal

As I attempted to leave Olveston, I somehow managed to take a wrong turn, ending up down the dead-end of a housing estate. After a quick u-turn, I managed to find the route and headed out towards the M48 and over the M4. I did consider heading through Bristol city centre. However, I thought of how busy the traffic would be and decided against it.

I continued my way down to Avonmouth, over the M5 bridge which has a footpath and cycleway running alongside it. Once over the bridge, I found myself heading around the perimeter of the car import centre. I had driven up and down the M5 countless times, and I always wondered about the hundreds of cars parked up down there.

Then, it was round to Portbury before heading southwest along the quiet road running way down below the M5 to Clevedon. From Clevedon, it was then south to Yatton. Here, I joined onto the Strawberry Line, once a disused railway line but since given a new lease of life as a beautiful path for cyclist and walkers to enjoy. This led me all the way down to Sandford.

So far, the route had been, for the most part, entirely flat, apart from some undulating terrain. What followed was a very steep climb up to the top of the Mendips to reach the campsite. As per usual, I had no energy left, and it was rather hot with the sun being out. As a result, I ended up pushing my bike most of the way up, finding myself getting angry with how long it seemed to take. When would it bloody end? And where was this campsite? I thought to myself.

Finally arriving, I just flopped down in the field, spread-eagled and soaked up the sun, relieved at reaching my destination once again. There were no facilities apart from a toilet block, but it was enough to accommodate me for the night. So, I set up my tarp against the fence and basked in the remaining sunlight and turned in for an early night.

Day 15
The Mendips to Exeter - 77.96 mi (125.46 km)

I woke up early, as was always the case when wild camping, and managed to pack everything away very quickly. I had finally learnt to stop fussing about so much when packing everything away. I settled on my final bag of rice and tuna for breakfast, which was not in the slightest bit appealing, but at least it would provide me with some much-needed energy. I had cycled 88 miles home from Bristol a few weeks prior as part of a training ride. Now that I was past Bristol and at the top of the Mendips, I thought it would be an easy run back to Exeter, providing a much-needed boost in motivation.

Leaving the campsite, it was thankfully a long descent into Cheddar along the Somerset Levels to the charming village of Wedmore. As I cycled through the village, my eyes immediately spotted the sign outside The Swan advertising coffees, so I decided to stop off for a morning coffee and summarise the route ahead. The previous time I rode from Bristol to Exeter, we headed over the Black Down Hills, towards Honiton. I settled on a flatter route this time, heading over to Bridgewater, along the canal path to Taunton, over to Tiverton, then down through the Exe Valley.

As expected, leaving Wedmore was a nice and easy flat section across the Somerset Levels passing through Cossington and Bawdrip. Once through Bawdrip, blindly following the sat nav, it wasn't until a mile after that I realised the road entered out onto the A39. I didn't particularly fancy riding on a busy A road, going at a slow pace. So, I about turned and rode back where I was supposed to turn off onto a path that ran alongside the King's Sedgemoor Drain, adding a mile or so to my journey. It was then on through Chedzoy, where I joined up to the River Parrett. Upon reaching Bridgewater, it was then another 14.5 miles to Taunton along the Bridgewater to Taunton Canal, a picturesque route and an excellent spot for walking.

When I finally made it to Taunton, I was going to take a rest stop at French Wear park, but with it being such a hot day in the middle of the week, the place was a hive of activity. So, I thought I would press on and find a shop to pick up some supplies. I feel I have to add that French Wear Park is the start of The Two Counties Way, a beautiful long-distance walk; starting in Taunton and finishing in Starcross, in the Exe Estuary.

From French Wier, I carried along the NCN route 3 passing through the grounds of Somerset College of Arts & Technology, where I went to college a few years prior. It was then on through Bishops Hull where I spotted a shop. So, I thought it'd be best to fuel up on cans of pop, a hot sausage roll, and two pastries before taking a break on the bench outside the shop. From here, the trail followed close by to the remnants of the canal that used to run from Tiverton to Taunton, passing through Nynehead.

Upon reaching Greenham, I joined back onto the Grand Western Canal, the section that is still in working order. Like the Bridgewater to Taunton canal, this section provides another lovely walk or cycle route as it meanders through the countryside, passing by the sleepy villages of Sampford Peverell and Halberton.

On passing through Halberton, I departed from the canal towpath. I headed along country lanes, cutting diagonally across to Butterleigh and entering out on to the A396, that runs between Tiverton and Exeter. This was one A road that I certainly didn't mind going on, as I've ridden down it so many times, I could practically ride it blindfolded. I always break the villages on this road into sections in my mind, so I know exactly how far I have left to go. My route then took me over the bridge at Stoke Canon, which is when I rounded the corner before making a left turn onto Pennsylvania Road for a 1.2-mile climb, the final hill of the day; not what you need after a 78-mile cycle ride. But it would bring me out close to my home.

Finally, I had made it back home. It was strange walking through the door, thinking that 16 days ago, I had set out on my epic adventure, and here I was back home. Like I had just been out on a long cycle. As soon as I walked in the door, I sprang into action to get everything sorted for the next morning.

With only two days left of cycling, I discarded anything that I no longer required to try and lighten the load. I plugged everything in that needed to be charged, put on a change of clothes, grabbed my road bike, and headed down the hill to Morrisons.

However, as I had been spending up to 10-11 hours a day on my mountain bike for the past 16 days, with its long bars and more upright riding position, I had lost my ability to ride a road bicycle. I was all over the road trying to find my balance.

After stocking up on lots of food for the evening and a few bits for the remainder of my journey, it was time to ascend the hill back to my flat. This was just not happening, I had accustomed myself to the extra gearing on my mountain bike, and I had nothing left in my legs after the long day, so I ended up walking the final 900 metres back.

Upon returning home, I loaded up on the calories. As I finally had access to a proper bicycle pump, I discovered to my horror, that my rear tyre only had a pressure of 20 psi! No wonder it felt like I had been riding through treacle, although they didn't seem flat. I did wonder if they had been like that since the slow puncture incident on Day 10. After a long hot shower, I assumed the horizontal position and fell into a deep sleep.

Day 16
Exeter to Dartmoor (Brentor) - 36.48 mi (58.70 km)

After having a fantastic night's sleep, I woke around 6:00 am, due to my routine of waking up early over the last few days. What followed was exactly what I knew would happen, which is why I initially decided against planning to stop at home. But, as I had managed to keep to the schedule, I had at least three days to spare before my train home that I had initially booked, plenty of time!

So, I laid in bed for a good few hours, constantly saying to myself, just another hour, just another thirty minutes. I eventually left my flat at around 12:15 pm. But I did use this time wisely, as I fuelled up on three pots of porridge, three cups of coffee, along with numerous cereal bars.

Leaving my flat, I used the same route I had taken to get to St David's station when I originally left. It did feel a little strange, as only a few days ago, I was heading along this route to set off for the other side of the country. But this time, I was to continue past St David's, over Exe bridges, and head up through the steep part of Exeter, Exwick. Initially, this involved a 4-mile climb before a descent into Ted Burn St Mary. Basically, following the NCN route 279. Before I set off, I figured this was my best route. I would have had to have conquered hills whatever the route, so I might as well take the more direct approach.

After passing the village of Tedburn, it was through into Whidden Down, then along to South Zeal, a combination of many more long hills and descents. The day was beautiful, the heat blistering, which made getting to Okehampton hard going. However, the spectacular views made it all worthwhile. Before I knew it, I had arrived in Okehampton which is situated on the northern plateau of Dartmoor and almost centrally in Devon.

Every time I visit Okehampton, I seem to end up visiting the café located at the train station. So of course, I had to factor in a rest stop and grab a bite to eat. Plus, it was also the start of the Granite Trail

Cycle Path; running between Okehampton to Lydford Gorge, the route I would be taking before heading over to Launceston.

While taking in some much-needed calories, I did ponder what cycling through Cornwall would be like. I was venturing into uncharted lands, not having explored further west, other than a couple of trips to Newquay in the past. I also had no accommodation booked for the evening, so I had to keep an eye out for a suitable location.

The station is also the start point of another long-distance walking route, the Devonshire Heartland Way; running from Okehampton to Stoke Canon, situated to the north of Exeter. As the name suggests, this is a beautiful trail through the very centre of Devon.

Okehampton railway station

From the station, I followed along the Granite trail down to Brentor, stopping at another café that formed part of an old train carriage overlooking the Meldon Aqueduct and reservoir. By this point, it was now getting into early evening, and so I decided it would be best to at least get past Lydford Gorge. The area to the south is open moorland, where you can legally wild camp. However, the area was completely devoid of trees to hook my tarp up against, while also being devoid of any phone signal. Despite this, I did consider pitching up against the stone wall.

In the end, as the weather was glorious, I wandered further up the hill, thinking I'd be able to get some sort of phone coverage the higher I went, but no. I could just about get one bar if I rested my phone on the handlebars and not touch it. Well, here I was, no cover and exposed to the elements. But the sky was beautiful, so I thought I'd take the risk and sleep under the stars. I rolled out my mat and sleeping bag and laid there, joyous to know that I only had a couple of days left to get through.

Day 17
Dartmoor (Brentor) to Veryan - 73.63 mi (118.49 km)

After a restful night's sleep under the stars, I awoke early to catch the sunrise and swiftly fell back to sleep again for another couple hours, not getting up until around 9 o'clock. So much for my plan on getting away early!

Even though I had a good night's sleep, I didn't have any motivation to carry on. Of course, I was going to finish it and get to the end, but it seemed the closer I got to the end, the harder it was to find any motivation.

Leaving the moorland, I made my way through Brentor, over to Chillaton, then through to the village of Lifton. Here, I stopped in the local shop to grab some breakfast and pulled up on the village green to relax for a few minutes. Lifton is right on the border, so I was very excited to be crossing over into the final county on this adventure. This was despite all that I had heard about Cornwall being bad for hills.

Crossing into Cornwall

From Lifton, it was down through to Launceston. On my way, I came across the Cornwall border sign. I certainly had to get a mandatory photo to mark the occasion. With cars following behind me, I slowed down, indicating I was going to stop. As I went to put my foot down, to my horror, there was no floor. So, down I went into the hidden ditch running alongside, partly hidden by the foliage. Luckily, I didn't entirely end up in the bushes, but my leg was scratched to pieces and bleeding from the thorns. I must have looked a right fool to the car behind.

Once through Launceston, I made my way north-west up through Egloskerry, over to Tresmeer then across to Hallworthy. It was just as they said, the hills were terrible! It reminded me a bit like the optical illusion where it appears the stairs are always leading upwards or downwards depending on how you look at the image because it seemed like I was continually heading uphill with hardly any descents.

Soon, I found myself passing through the remnants of Bodmin Airfield. Here, I faced a monumental battle with the most ferocious headwind I have ever encountered. Glad to get as far away from the airfield as possible, I continued along winding backroads until I joined up with the camel trail which leads all the way into Bodmin.

My original plan was to go back to following the book, heading in the direction of Newquay, then down to Truro. However, this was a considerable distance, so I looked at the alternative of heading through St Austell, getting the ferry crossing at Trelissick Landing further on. In my mind, this seemed a much better idea as it was a far shorter distance.

After the switch in my planned route, the race was on to catch the last ferry crossing at 10:30 pm. At my current rate, this was a mammoth task, as I still had 12 miles (20 km) to cover. On a standard road bike, this would have been easy. But as always, with the terrain, it was hard going. While heading along a country lane, an open gate leading into a field caught my eye. The darkness was fast approaching, and I thought if I left it any later, then it would have been more of a hassle setting up camp.

I pulled into the field to have a look. I propped my bike up against the fence and sat on the damp floor, not wanting to set my tarp up, paranoid that a tractor would come bounding through the entrance at any second.

After a few minutes, I thought the field opposite might be better. It had some sort of vegetables growing, so I thought that no one would be out here at this time of night. Plus, there was a closed gate across the entrance. As it was now dark, I made my move, entering the adjacent field and scooting along the hedge line about 50-60 metres.

The sky was overcast, but I thought I would risk not getting the tarp out as I didn't want kit all over the place, just in case I needed to be off on my toes in a hurry.

Here I was laid in my sleeping bag, in a massive tractor tyre track, surrounded by cabbages, with brambles to the right of me. Due to the sheer number of thorns, my roll matt stood no chance. Inevitably, it was soon flat as a pancake, probably riddled with holes.

As I lay there, the patter of rain started. Not tonight! I quickly leapt into action and hastily erected a shocking attempt at a shelter, with my kit all over the place. There was nothing to hook the bungees around to tie off the end of the tarp. So, I tried to loop them around the brambles and got scratched to pieces in the process.

I crawled back into my sleeping bag and didn't hear any more rain, which led me to wonder if I was just being paranoid the first time around. Anyway, I was here now. As I laid back down to try and get some sleep, a few minutes later, a car arrived at the gate, headlights illuminating the whole area. My God, I thought, they're coming in! It was the farmer, and I presume his wife had come back from an evening out. One of them got out to open the gate to drive into the field.

It happened to be the entrance to a long drive leading up to a farm beyond the hill in the distance. All I could think was please God, don't let them see me. Thankfully, nobody did. As it was private property, I was left slightly paranoid, if they were to leave early in the morning then surely, they would see me. So, I ended up packing everything up and moved back to the original field and spent the night just in my sleeping bag on my roll mat with multiple puncture wounds. Thankfully, it never did rain.

Day 18
Veryan to Land's End - 53.51 mi (86.11 km)

After the night's comedic performance, I woke early after getting about 3 hours of sleep. Every time I wild camped, there were usually two characteristic features, a terrible night's sleep and the inability to get out of my snug sleeping bag. This time, however, I was up with kit packed away in seconds. The main reason for this being that today was the final day of this monumental journey. The thought of being home for good tonight was undoubtedly enough motivation to get me going.

Leaving the field, it was a short distance down into the charming village of Veryan, what a great place this small village would have been to camp, I thought. It was then on down to King Harry Ferry Crossing. When I arrived at the crossing, it was all very quiet, I thought. Upon checking the large sign, I discovered I got the timings of the first ferry wrong. It was, of course, a Sunday, and the ferries started running an hour later. So, I propped my bike up against the wall, took a seat on the curb, and had breakfast - a bag of Haribo.

Closer to the time the ferry was due to run, another cyclist joined me. He was a guy who had recently relocated to the area from South Africa. We had a friendly chat, and once we reached the other side, he sped off on his way, while I slowly made my way through Carnon Downs and over to Four Lanes. Here, I popped into the local shop and bought more food. I don't remember much of this section, as I was just concentrating on digging in and moving forward.

I gave up on following the book again, as I wasn't in the mood for scenic detours, I was just following Google Map's recommendation, still following the quieter roads. I passed on through Praze-an-Beeble, Leedstown then over to St Erth. From here, I headed southwest down to Marazion, thinking it was Penzance. I stopped by the wall, and I felt a little emotional. Although I still had a way to go before the finish line, I thought I was so close.

I pressed on not wanting to hang about too long and made my way, this time, around to Penzance. Then, I thought I might start to follow the book again. The route took me around to Mousehole and over to St Buryan. What a mistake! As the going was tough, and hills were brutal. As soon as I would get to the top, it would be downhill straight into the next incline, many of which I walked up.

However, after passing through St Buryan, I was ever so close. I had passed through Trevescan, now on the home straight. As soon as I saw Land's End's car park, the biggest smile covered my face!

Looking over to St Michael's Mount

I raced to the ticket booths, a guy waved me straight through and told me to proceed directly ahead, following the road that leads down to the iconic building and the final couple hundred metres. Here, I slowed right down to a crawl to savour the last hundred metres, as I was thinking about the journey I had just completed, I had made it!

A grass bank opposite from the entrance of the main building looked very appealing, so I sat down with a huge smile still gleaming across my face, trying to comprehend what I had just accomplished. The whole complex was heaving with people, although that is probably not surprising, with it being a sunny Sunday in the middle of the school holidays.

After a few minutes rest, I wanted to have a look around the area and of course, find the sign to get my picture taken. This was an extraordinary moment, so I thought it would be a nice memento to hang up on the wall. After standing line for about 25 minutes, it was my turn. I opted for 'Matt's JOGLE, 8th-25th August'. Afterwards, several people came up to me and asked questions, with one guy even wanting to have his picture taken with me.

It was then round to the hotel, where inside the foyer there is a logbook that you can sign which is full of people's names who have completed or are setting off on LEOG/JOGLE. I proceeded to the café for a bite to eat, opting for a chicken burger and chips, which was rather disgusting. Why I didn't choose a pasty, being in Cornwall, I do not know. I also had a celebratory pint of Cornish cider.

Made it to Land's End!

But, as had always been the case, there wasn't long to hang around. The time had come to turn around and cycle the 12 miles (19 km) back to the station in Penzance to catch the 7:00 pm train; I chose a route that was a lot shorter and flatter than following the NCN route out from Penzance, arriving at the station with an hour to spare.

All in all, I found arriving at the finish line had been all rather anticlimactic, apart from a huge smile, I didn't have any feelings of elation. Perhaps it hadn't yet sunk in properly? Either way, I was pleased that I had made it, later learning I had covered over 1100 miles, and thankful it was over.

Final Stats

Distance: 1123.05 miles

Moving Time: 119:35:27

Elevation: 17,627 m

FINISHING JOGLE

When I arrived back at Exeter St David's, I got up to leave the train, discovering that I was in a lot of pain. After sitting relaxed for the 3-hour journey home, my body had decided to start hurting, probably after all the abuse it had endured over the previous days. I had some real painful saddle sores, and I could hardly walk as my knee was so painful. Even though I was back in Exeter, I still had to get home to my flat on the other side of town. I did not enjoy the final 2-mile (3.2km) cycle.

As soon as I opened the door, it was now finally over. I parked my bike up, sorted all my kit out, took a very long time in the shower, and ordered a celebratory takeaway. I was proud of my victorious achievement and thrilled knowing that I could get a fantastic night's sleep and not need to get up early in the morning.

Over the next couple of days, I experienced a small sense of sadness. I actually missed the routine of getting up and setting off to a different place. The next day, even though I still woke up at the crack of dawn and no longer sore, I did think about going for a cycle. It felt kind of weird not being on a bike, as I had spent between 10-12 hours in the saddle each day for the past eighteen days. But I decided against it and made the most of my comfy bed, reminiscing on my journey and incredible experience; to have ridden the length of the United Kingdom the hardest way possible.

I had a further two days off before I had to be back into work - going back to my commute which involved a 4 mile walk each day, a mile of which involves a very steep hill which I just couldn't bear to think about. So, for about a month, I ended up getting the bus from the train station to my workplace. My body had just crashed, so I didn't do anything for a long time afterwards. Likewise, I found myself eating excessively after I had finished due to my higher metabolism. All the weight I had lost was soon put back on; although it would have been interesting to know how much I weighed before and after.

So, unless you're some kind of masochist, someone who enjoys the gratification from their pain, then cycling End to End is going to be seriously tough, both mentally and physically. As along the way, you'll likely have to endure wild camping, ride against headwinds, endure torrential downpours, all while on a bike.

Nevertheless, what a fantastic experience it was. Riding the breadth of the United Kingdom was indeed one of the greatest adventures and achievements of my life. To experience the changing landscapes of the country, how each county has its unique features and beautiful villages was a real pleasure. Not forgetting everyone who stopped by for a chat and those who helped me out, it made my experience a whole lot more special.

AFTER THOUGHTS

LEJOG is for wimps

Only joking, riding any such distance is going to be tough. However, riding 60-70 miles a day, fighting against the prevailing winds does present its challenges. I can see why most people take the easier option of cycling LEJOG.

Cornwall is Hilly

Everyone says Cornwall is the hilliest part and how right they are! Being from Devon, I certainly know a few hills, but I didn't find Devon to be that bad when I passed through. It seems Cornwall has all the hills though and was undoubtedly the hardest cycling I'd ever done. Or maybe it was because I was getting close to the end and was so exhausted. With the constant up and down of the hills, it was really slow going.

Wild Camping

Don't wild camp, unless you want to punish yourself. Every time I wild camped, I suffered a horrible night's sleep, tossing and turning all night, usually only grabbing 2-3 hours as my roll mat was so uncomfortable. But it did offer a unique experience. But not one I'd repeat any time soon, might I add!

Mountain Bike

OK, so a mountain bike might not be the best choice of bike. If you want to make life easier for yourself, a bike with thinner tyres might be the way to go. Even though I swapped out the original knobbly tyres for smooth touring ones, for better rolling resistance, as soon as I stopped pedalling, I'd quickly come to a stop. Every mile was like a spinning workout.

Recovery

Make time for recovery. They say it takes about 26 days to recover from a marathon. So, who knows how long it would take for your body to fully recover after cycling 1000+ miles. I went from cycling 60-80 miles a day to completely stopping, and my body crashed, so much I struggled on my morning commute. It took me a couple of months before I got back on a bike.

"I've always wanted to give it a go."

If you've ever thought about doing it, stop thinking about it and do it! Don't wait for the right opportunity, whether that be retirement or a couple of years from now to properly plan, because there will never be a right time. I planned, trained (kind of), and completed my journey all within seven months.

Printed in Great Britain
by Amazon

81502621R00056